Sand & Soil

Sand & Soil

Creating Beautiful Gardens on Cape Cod and the Islands

C. L. FORNARI

For Dan, again and always. Because of you,
all our gardens have thrived.

Published in 2019 by
David R. Godine, Publisher, Inc.
Post Office Box 450
Jaffrey, New Hampshire 03452
www.godine.com

Library of Congress Cataloging-in-Publication Data

Names: Fornari, C. L. (Cynthia Lynn), 1950- author.
Title: Sand and soil : Creating Beautiful Gardens on Cape Cod and the Islands /
by C.L. Fornari.
Description: Boston, Massachusetts : David R. Godine, Publisher, 2019. |
Includes bibliographical references and index.
Identifiers: LCCN 2018047259 | ISBN 9781567926415 (hardcover with color
illustrations throughout : alk. paper)
Subjects: LCSH: Sandy soil gardening--Massachusetts--Cape Cod. | Sandy soil
gardening--Massachusetts--Martha's Vineyard. | Sandy soil
gardening--Massachusetts--Nantucket Island. | Seaside
gardening--Massachusetts--Cape Cod. | Seaside
gardening--Massachusetts--Martha's Vineyard. | Seaside
gardening--Massachusetts--Nantucket Island.
Classification: LCC SB459.6 .F676 2019 | DDC 635.9/550974494--dc23
LC record available at https://lccn.loc.gov/2018047259

FIRST EDITION 2019
Printed in China

Contents

Introduction

WHEN I MOVED TO CAPE COD in 1993 my friend Wendy said, "Oh good…now you can grow those *outrageous* blue hydrangeas." And sure enough, blue mopheads and lacecaps were among the first plants I purchased for our house in Osterville. Twenty-five years later these shrubs also play a big role in my gardens in Sandwich, where they thrive along with hundreds of other plants. It has been a delightful adventure to discover how to work with the Cape's soil and weather, and I've enjoyed discovering the variety of plants that grow well near the sea.

What's been equally enjoyable and totally surprising has been my cultivation of a wonderful community of homeowners and fellow gardeners. When I came to the Cape I'd been working as an artist for years, with no thought of being a garden communicator. I've always been a gardener, however, and when we moved here I looked for a book about gardening in this region, only to find that there wasn't one. This set me down the path that ultimately led to eight books, radio programs, landscape consulting, and public speaking. Life takes us all in unexpected directions, and I am blessed that my path led into gardens.

Since my first book, *The Cape Cod Garden*, was released, several things in landscaping have changed. New pests and diseases have arrived in the region, presenting area gardeners with assorted challenges. We've seen changes in weather as well, as summers have gotten hotter while our springs seem just as ephemeral as always.

Plants such as barberry (*Berberis*) and burning bush (*Euonymus alatus*), standardly planted in many yards and gardens when I came to the Cape, are now illegal to sell in the state of Massachusetts. Other plants, such as Leyland cypress, that seemed like a good choices in 1993 have proven to be problematic for many landscapes. Yet hundreds of other worthy plants have been introduced so Cape and Island gardeners have access to a larger palette for planting than ever before.

As I've visited scores of Cape and Island gardens over the past twenty-five years, I've seen which plants grow well here and which varieties sulk or are likely to die. This book contains more of the former. While there are many worthy plants that thrive in other regions, they aren't mentioned in this book because they don't flourish here, are high maintenance, or are chronically prone to problems.

Other changes I've seen over the past twenty-five years include access to more organic solutions to problems, and changes in our thinking about fertilization. For example, when I moved to Cape Cod it was a common practice to throw a handful of super phosphate in the ground when planting perennials; now we know that phosphorous is a pollutant that should never be routinely put into gardens. Similarly, at that time it was customary to amend shrub and tree planting holes with one part peat moss, one part manure, and one part native soil. Now we know that such soil amendments actually create reduced root systems. So our knowledge about plants, products, and practices continues to expand.

My hope is that the information in this book will help home landscapers and gardeners to not only be successful in their yards and gardens, but to be inspired as well. To that end the majority of photos in this book are of gardens, not of specific plants or problems, and those gardens range from modest to elaborate. The pictures in this book contain take-away information and ideas for Cape and Island residents of all levels of landscape and garden experience.

Cape Cod, Martha's Vineyard, and Nantucket are exceptional locations for cultivating beautiful landscapes. We live in a special region, close to scenic waterways, refreshed by sea breezes, and surrounded with greenery. It is the perfect location for creating lovely landscapes, and of course for growing those outrageous blue hydrangeas.

Gardening By The Sea ~
Soils and Weather

GARDEN WRITERS ARE FOND of saying "All gardening is regional." Although we recognize that many aspects of plants and gardening remain the same from one place to the other, it's also true that each location has unique growing conditions. Soil and weather create environments that support

It is typical for houses on the Cape and Islands to have a clapboard front with shutters on the windows, but shingles on the sides and back of the building. This style has proved practical as painted or stained surfaces age faster in our humid air. But beyond architecture, the styles of our landscapes vary tremendously.

specific plants and encourage distinctive types of growth. It is these regional conditions that let us grow spectacular *Rhododendron* shrubs on the Cape and Islands, but don't allow us to raise the large crape myrtles that flourish in Georgia, or the sculptural blue *Agave* that do well in the west.

On the Cape and Islands, our soils, temperatures, rainfall and wind determine the palette of plants we use and how well they will grow. These same conditions, along with the shingle-covered houses, are what give our regional landscapes their panache. It is the plants and how they are combined that makes our landscapes look like distinctive Cape Cod, Martha's Vineyard, or Nantucket gardens.

Beyond appearances, however, the way we deal with the native soils and cope with changes in weather influences our success or failure in the landscape. There are environmental conditions that we can change, and others where control isn't possible. Cultivating landscapes on the Cape and Islands is largely a matter of starting with what you've got, changing what you can, and working with all that can't be controlled.

Chapter 1 *Soils*

GLACIAL DEPOSITS LEFT after the retreat of the Laurentide ice sheet some 18,000 years ago created Cape and Island soils. The rock debris deposited by glaciers ranges from very fine silt to sand, clay, and rocks of all sizes, from pebbles to boulders. This means that the quality of the soil varies tremendously from one area to the next. Some find heavy clay when they dig, while others encounter pure beach sand. There are stretches of silt-rich loam, areas filled with a jumble of rocks and soil, and places containing layers of all of the above.

For those planting landscapes and gardens in this region, it's important to know what soil type you're starting with. Soil type determines what plants will grow well, how to best maintain those plantings, and how to improve this environment moving forward.

Many on the Cape and Islands plant in beach sand. While some plants such as these Rosa rugosa *seem to thrive in such dry conditions, most of our landscape plants need better soil.*

SAND, CLAY OR LOAM There are three ways to determine what kind of soil you're dealing with: sight, touch and the Mason jar test. Sight is easy but not very precise. Dig a hole that's at least a foot deep and take a look at what's there. Often the top layer is darker because plants have been decomposing in the area and enriching the surface over time. There might even be roots, bits of composting leaves and pieces of bark or stems. But the bottom of the hole is more likely to show the native soil.

If the bottom of the hole contains grains that look like the beach, you've got sand. In some areas this sand is close to the surface as well. If the bottom of the hole contains dark soil that is fairly easy to dig in, you're fortunate to have loam. And if the bottom of the hole is harder to dig it might be clay. In this area clay soils can be gray, reddish, or even tan in color.

Dig a small scoop of soil from the bottom of the hole and feel it. Sand and a sandy loam will feel grainy. If the sample is moist, squeeze it into a small ball. When you open your hand, the sand won't stay in that ball for long. Loam will keep the shape until poked with a finger, at which point it falls apart unless it's quite wet or rich with organic material. Clay that's squeezed into a ball will retain that shape even when prodded.

Another way to judge the quality of your soil is to measure out a cup of soil and put it into a Mason jar. Fill the jar almost to the top with water and add one drop of dishwashing soap after the water is added. Cap the jar and gently turn it upside down and back a couple of times. Avoid shaking the jar as that will produce suds from the soap. Place the jar on a level surface and watch what happens. Sand sinks to the bottom of the jar almost immediately. If you see almost a full cup of sand at the bottom of your jar after five minutes, you've got more sand than anything else, no matter what color it was before it went into the jar. Finer particles of silt settle next.

Leave the jar untouched for an hour or two and see how large the layer on top of the sand is. Clay settles after silt, followed or accompanied by any waterlogged organic matter. Some organic matter will stay floating on the top of the water. This method allows you to roughly judge what percentage of sand, silt, clay and organic matter your sample contains.

SAND Sandy soils dry rapidly and aren't as nutrient rich. The air spaces between grains of sand ensure that the water runs through the soil swiftly. In practical terms for the landscaper and gardener, this means that sandy soils dry quickly, and the water takes added nutrients with it. So sandy soils aren't as rich in nitrogen and other nutrients. On the plus side, many plants thrive in well-drained soil, so once the native sand is amended with organic matter it is often a foundation for good growth.

Organic matter improves sandy soils because it acts like tiny sponges that hold both water and nutrients. So the most important strategy for dealing with sand is a liberal use of organic amendments. If your yard is primarily sand, compost and composted manure will be your savior. These can be dug into new beds and applied on the surface of existing plantings. Mulch, compost and composted manure all amend soils from the top down. Over time the annual addition of such organics will improve sandy soils significantly.

Planting in sandy soils is partly a matter of adding amendments. But in areas where the ground is pure sand, it's also important to choose plants that normally cope well in this soil type. Look for native plants that grow well in wild areas such as bayberry (*Myrica pensylvanica*), inkberry (*Ilex glabra*), bearberry (*Archtostaphylos uva-ursi*) and yucca (*Yucca filamentosa*). But just because a plant grows well in the woods or by the beach, that doesn't mean it's native to the area. The wild rose (*Rosa multiflora*) and bittersweet (*Celastrus orbiculatus*), for example, are wild and invasive, and the common beach rose (*Rosa rugosa*) is very aggressive.

The soil in this Vineyard garden has been regularly amended with organic matter for many years. This has made the top twelve inches darker, but as the shovel digs down the sandy nature of the topsoil is revealed.

LOAM Loam is a fairly even mix of sand, silt, clay and organic matter. While most people have soils that swing toward more sand or a predominance of clay, a few lucky folks on the Cape and Islands have an ideal mixture of particle sizes. For growing plants, this is like winning the lottery. Loam still benefits from the regular addition of organic matter on the soil's surface, but a thin layer of mulch, chopped leaves, or an inch of compost or aged manure can easily accomplish this.

CLAY Clay holds onto moisture longer, which is helpful during times of drought. It also is more nutrient rich than sand. Paradoxically, the same treatment that is used to make sandy soils more fertile and moist is used to lighten clay soils. Adding compost or composted manure is the key to inserting the air spaces that make clay soils drain better. Organic matter can be dug into new beds and layered on the top of the soil around existing plantings. Do not try and improve clay soils by adding sand; this produces a mixture that resembles cement.

Knowing the value of constantly adding organic matter to the soil, Dave and Sandy Light have local landscapers drop off leaves that are used as mulch and soil amendments in their Orleans market garden.

On Martha's Vineyard there are areas of pure sand, sandy loam, clay and mixes of all of those. This garden, designed by Carly Look with stonework by Lew French, makes artful use of the soil, plants and rocks.

IMPROVING THE NATIVE SOIL: MULCH & OTHER AMENDMENTS

Improving soils is best accomplished just as nature does it: from the top down, with organic matter that decomposes into the ground. Chopped leaves, seaweed, manure, bark mulches, pine needles and compost are all good soil amendments. An inch-thick layer of bark mulch, manure or compost every year is sufficient. Other materials such as leaf pieces, seaweed and pine needles can be spread up to three inches thick since they settle over time, but more mulch isn't better. The roots of existing plants need a combination of the soil, organic matter, moisture and air to do well; too much mulch prevents roots from getting the air they need. A thick layer of mulch will also absorb all of the moisture in shallow rainfalls or brief periods of irrigation, preventing the water from reaching the plants' roots. When it comes to soil amendments, moderation is best.

Many wonder if bark mulch is a landscape necessity since its use has become fairly ubiquitous in the last thirty years. Although mulch is not essential, there are many reasons for using it in Cape and Island gardens. Mulch is useful for retaining moisture, preventing weed seeds from germinating, and amending the soil from the top down. But mulch doesn't have to be bark or wood chips although these are commonly available. Chopped leaves would work just as well to accomplish all of those goals. Seaweed can be used as mulch but it's likely to be uneven and a bit messy in appearance, not to mention harder to spread into small spaces.

Mulch color doesn't make any difference, and cedar mulches do not keep insects away. Choose the type of mulching material that suits your budget and design preferences, keeping in mind that finer mulches are best for preventing weed growth and retaining ground moisture.

SEAWEED, OAK LEAVES & PINE NEEDLES These are three soil amendments that many on the Cape and Islands have free access to. Check with your local town about their policy for removing seaweed from a beach before you go to collect it, however. Leaves and pine needles should only be gathered from your own property, never from open or conservation lands.

Most seaweed piles are a combination of true seaweed, eelgrass, and the stems of beach grass or other plants. These can all be used to enrich soils but the seaweed breaks down fastest. Note that the amount of salt on seaweed isn't usually too significant. If it makes you feel better to rinse it, by

ABOVE: *The Abate garden on Cape Cod looks as if the entire front yard is a garden bed. Actually, there are grass paths in between strips of narrow flowerbeds.*

LEFT: *The grass paths cut the work of weeding and mulching in half while adding easy access for tending the flowerbeds. These perennial gardens are mulched which serves three purposes. Mulch keeps down weeds, helps retain soil moisture, and amends the beds with organic matter as the mulching materials break down.*

LEFT: *Compost can be spread around a plant at any time. An inch or two spread over the surface of the soil is ideal, especially if it covers an entire bed or well past the plants' drip-lines.*

BELOW: *Compost can be shoveled out over the surface of a lawn. This is especially effective after the turf is aerated in the fall, although it can be done in the spring as well. If desired, seed can be sown in bare areas after the compost is spread.*

all means do so. But usually in the time the piles of seaweed have sat on the beach it has been rinsed by rain.

It is a myth that oak leaves and pine needles make soil acidic. Here in the Northeast we have acidic soils from the natural mineral composition and, to some extent, because of acid rain. When organic matter breaks down, pH comes to near neutral, even if it was acidic before decomposing. So don't hesitate to use those oak leaves and pine needles as mulch or compost for your gardens. Chop leaves with a lawn mower or chipper so that they don't blow around and spread more easily. Alternatively, pile them and let the leaves compost for a year until they are dark and crumbly.

TOWN COMPOST Many wonder about the wisdom of using of compost that is available for free at many town transfer stations. Although it is true that it's impossible to tell if they contain residue of products such as herbicides and insecticides, the likelihood is that the quantities of such substances are small. Town composts become fairly homogenized in the turning and blending process. To be on the safe side, however, most people won't use this compost on their vegetable gardens, and those who stick solely to organic methods won't want to use it at all. My opinion is that for those on a budget, an application of town compost on lawns, or around shrubs, trees and ornamental plants is better than no organic matter at all.

I've seen the application of town compost make a significant difference when applied on sandy, sparse lawns. Once, a consultation client spread just under an inch over most of her turf, but ran out before the backyard was covered. There was a clear line down the center of her yard; on one side was the thicker, green lawn that the compost had promoted. On the side that didn't get compost, the exposed sand and sparse tufts of grass remained.

PURCHASED LOAM Those starting new landscapes might need to purchase loam, but the success of this method depends on what they are starting with, what they intend to grow, how quickly they need to plant, and the quality of the loam. Loam is most helpful when the native soil is very sandy and a traditional lawn and landscaping are planned. In this case, a six to eight inch layer of good quality loam works well.

The quality of a loam can be determined using the Mason jar test. [see page 6] Since loams come from various locations, they range from a well-balanced mix of soil particles to dark-colored sand. Needless to say, there is no reason for someone who has sandy soils to pay money for a darker version of what they already have.

CHANGING SOIL FERTILITY This author is biased toward organic methods. Organic fertilizers nourish plants in much the same way as nature does, so to my mind it makes sense to use them when such amendments are needed. But I also believe that the occasional use of synthetic fertilizers has its place, especially when it comes to growing annuals and plants in containers.

Before applying fertilizers in the landscape, have a soil test done. The University of Massachusetts soil testing lab in Amherst has a website that contains complete instructions for sampling soils and sending them in for analysis. Test results will contain the current nutrient levels in the soil as well as the existing pH or soil acidity. Never assume that you know how fertile or acidic the soil in any particular area is, and plan to have soil tested every three years. Soil nutrients may have been influenced by previous applications of fertilizer, and the pH can be raised by applications of lime or even the use of town water.

Since some plants require specific growing conditions it's smart to have separate tests done for lawns, vegetable gardens and areas where acid-loving plants such as Rhododendrons and blueberries are grown. A soil test is also the first step when diagnosing problems as well, so additional samples should be taken from around plants that aren't thriving.

Another reason for testing soil before fertilizing is that regulations for the application of phosphorous fertilizers have changed in the state of Massachusetts. Since excess phosphorous is one of the major pollutants of waterways, it's now illegal to apply phosphorous-containing fertilizers to lawns and gardens unless a soil test shows that you're deficient in this nutrient. This means no routine use of products with high middle numbers on the bag, or applications of "super phosphate."

Additional state restrictions that are important include a ban on applying fertilizers between December 1st and March 1st, spreading onto saturated or frozen soils, or use within twenty feet of a waterway. So whether you're using organic fertilizers or synthetic products, begin with a soil sample and act according to state and local laws.

LEFT: *Raised beds, like this one on the DeMelo property, need periodic refreshing with compost or a mix of compost and loam.*

BELOW: *This charming front yard is the home of Jose and Arlene DeMelo, founders of DeMelo Brothers Land-scaping. Much of the summer color on this property comes from annuals, and these plants perform best when they are regularly fertilized.*

The Sarcione garden consists of front beds planted with shrubs, perennials and trees.
Mulch is used in bare areas between the plants to suppress weed germination.

Timing of Fertilization & Soil Amendment Applications

Beyond regional mandates, the timing of fertilizer applications is important. Once you know that your soil would be improved by fertilization, it should be applied when plants can make best use of the nutrients. Organic fertilizers take six or more weeks to break down and become available to plants, and they continue to feed over time. For these reasons it makes sense to apply such products in March, April or early May. This timing ensures that the nutrients will be available in summer when the plants are actively growing.

By the same token, it doesn't make sense to apply granular organic fertilizers in July, August or September. Some liquid organic fertilizers become available to plants more quickly, so adding these to a vegetable garden in mid-summer is fine. Synthetic fertilizers are available more rapidly but again, they will be most efficiently used when used during the prime growing months of May and June. With the exception of a lawn, it's best not to give plants a synthetic fertilizer in the fall since during this season plants aren't putting on new growth.

Organic soil amendments such as compost, composted manure, chopped leaves and bark mulch can be spread on the soil just about anytime the

This lovely front garden was designed by horticulturalists George and Marcia Chapman. It shows that a foundation planting doesn't have to be a lineup of "the usual suspects."

ground isn't frozen. But a good schedule for fertilizing and amending Cape and Islands landscapes is to apply granular organic fertilizers where needed in the spring, and spread soil amendments in the fall. Synthetic fertilizers can be used in the growing season as needed on a plant-by-plant basis. Lawns have their own scheduling for fertilizers and soil amendments; see chapter 15.

Chapter 2 *Weather*

WHEN TALKING ABOUT PLANTS you'll frequently see zone designations about hardiness. These indicate where the plant will live through the winter's cold and the summer's heat. These zones are references to the USDA's Plant Hardiness Map, which divides areas of the United States into ten-degree Fahrenheit zones based on how low the temperatures go during winter. The difference between, say, zero and ten degrees Fahrenheit is significant, and the map doesn't distinguish between a place where the temperatures briefly touch on five degrees or those where entire days can be spent at that temperature. Additionally, factors such as moisture and wind play a role in whether plants are hardy. So these Hardiness Zones are a bit misleading and provide rough guidelines only.

Although the USDA map shows most of Cape Cod to be a cold Zone 7, or 7a, most plants said to grow well in that zone don't thrive here. Nantucket and Martha's Vineyard tend to be a bit more moderate, so some plants that are rated as Zone 7 do well on the Islands. And in all locations the closer you are to the ocean, the more moderate the temperatures, so the higher the likelihood that a Zone 7 plant will live. Nevertheless, if you want to be

The first heavy frost in this region often arrives in October, but low-lying areas might have a killing frost earlier because cold air sinks.

sure a plant will live through the winter, look for plants that are hardy in Zone 6 and below.

In terms of frosts, our last hard freeze in the spring is usually in early May, and the fall's killing frost comes in mid to late October. But since our nighttime temperatures stay so cold in the spring it's advisable to consider the end of May as the safe time for planting summer annuals and vegetables.

OCEAN EFFECTS Why some plants do better than others in any given location isn't just a matter of low winter temperatures. Several aspects of climate, along with other conditions particular to a location, can influence whether a plant grows well or struggles. In this region, the sea has a profound effect on our landscapes even if we don't garden on oceanfront properties.

When I first moved to the Cape I had the notion that only salt-tolerant plants would thrive in my Osterville gardens. I imagined that salt-spray would be an issue, even though I lived about a half-mile from the beach. I soon learned that salt damage is mainly a problem after hurricanes and some nor'easters. Normal winds might pick up some trace amounts of salt that get deposited on plants growing in oceanfront yards and gardens, but unless the winds are unusually strong and sustained, salt isn't carried too far.

Even more important than salt spray is the profound effect the ocean has on our temperatures. Because this large body of water holds onto the winter temperatures for months, we have colder springs on the Cape and Islands. When I first moved to Osterville I was told that, "On Cape Cod we have January, February, March, March, March, June." And sometimes June can be dicey.

We bless those off-ocean breezes in the summer, however. We might shiver in April or May while the rest of the state walks around in shirtsleeves, but we enjoy cooler summers while inland residents swelter. Later in the fall the ocean is well warmed from the long days of sunshine, and this keeps us warmer in through autumn. So at the end of the year we enjoy "September, September, September, December."

What does this mean for plants and gardens? Practically, these cold springs dictate that we can't plant many annuals and vegetables until late May. Although some planting guides advise people to look for the average date of last frost in the spring, on the Cape and Islands it's equally important to consider the overall temperature range. The soil in this region stays cold longer, and the nighttime temperatures can be chilly enough to do damage to summer plants. The general rule of thumb in this part of Massachusetts is that we wait to plant summer flowers and vegetables such as tomatoes, eggplant and basil until the night temperatures are *reliably above fifty degrees.* In most years this happens during the third or fourth week in May.

The cool spring weather isn't as problematic for planting shrubs and trees, but temperatures affect even their availability in nurseries if the stock is coming from warmer areas. It's usually safe to plant shrubs and trees as soon as they appear in area garden centers. But if the stock in the nursery looks drastically accelerated from what you see in the landscapes, there is a danger that those new plants might get cold damage or frosted.

Warm autumn temperatures, on the other hand, mean that summer annuals are often in flower, and vegetable gardens are producing through October. Many hydrangeas retain their blossoms until hard frost, and late-

In this lovely Nantucket garden that was planted and maintained by Chris and Buzz Hestwood, June-flowering perennials such as salvia (Salvia nemorosa) *and lady's mantle* (Alchemilla mollis) *mingle with self-seeding bread poppies* (Papaver somniferum) *and* Verbena bonariensis.

The sea breezes keep us cool, wave our flags, and create movement in our ornamental grasses, but they can also be hard on plants. On windy days plants lose more water through their leaves (transpiration) than when the air is calm. This hydrangea-filled landscape was created by Mal and Mary Kay Condon.

flowering perennials such as Nippon daisies and perennial mums are often in bloom into November. So whether we're appreciating our gardens, biking or golfing, the ocean delivers the warmer fall weather we enjoy.

WIND Salt-spray aside, wind has a significant effect on plants growing on the Cape and Islands. In all seasons the constant flow of air pulls moisture out of plants' leaves. Winter winds desiccate foliage because frozen soils don't allow roots to draw up water to replace what is being lost. In the summer, when plants naturally lose water through the pores of their leaves, the wind accelerates this process of transpiration. This is how plants keep cool in hot weather. Wind dries soils as well, especially on sunny days in the summer.

Frequent winds from one direction can bend plants and stunt their growth. Some withstand this stress better than others. In this region it's quite common for gusts to blow between thirty and sixty miles per hour during storms, causing leaves, twigs and branches to fall on our landscapes. Top-heavy pitch pine trees (*Pinus rigida*) often snap off midway up their trunks in such squalls. Even tall perennials can be flattened during storms in late summer and fall.

Most yards and gardens in this region have sections that are wind tunnels and other places that are protected from these gusts. Identifying where the winds hit and which areas are sheltered is important for placing plants in places where they will thrive.

RAIN & IRRIGATION   As long as I've lived on the Cape the rainfall has varied from year to year. One summer we might receive regular precipitation while the next year could be very dry. What established landscapes need to support their health and growth is an inch of rainfall a week, as measured in a rain gauge. A rain gauge is calibrated to measure a cubic inch of water falling on a square inch of ground. A tuna can, pail or wheelbarrow doesn't measure rainfall in the same way because the opening isn't equivalent to a square inch. You'll notice that on rain gauges that have larger openings on top, the one-inch mark is higher than an actual inch on the tube. That's because that larger measurement takes the larger opening into consideration. The bottom line is that seeing four inches of water in your wheelbarrow or pail does not mean we've received four inches of rainfall.

Every homeowner should have a rain gauge in the yard. It's important to have an accurate idea of what nature has delivered for a few reasons. First, knowing that established plants have gotten an inch or more of water tells you that you don't have to haul out the hose or turn on your sprinkler system for at least seven days. Newly germinated seedlings, or larger plants recently placed in the garden, might need watering more frequently in hot weather, but mature plants have large enough root systems to keep them healthy even if the top few inches of the soil dries up.

When watering plants with sprinklers or automatic systems, it's once again important to emulate how nature waters. Far too many systems are set up to run every other day for fifteen or twenty minutes. This is the opposite of how Mother Nature delivers moisture, and it's bad for plants. Yes, even the lawn.

Given only fifteen or twenty minutes of watering, only the top two or three inches of the soil will be soaked. In mulched beds this distance will be even less because mulch absorbs much of the water. If the top two or three inches of a lawn or planting bed are all that is being saturated, where will those plants' root systems be? In the irrigated soil, of course. So frequent, shallow watering tends to create turf, shrubs, and other plants with insubstantial roots.

Additionally, the frequent splashing of water on foliage is a prescription for fungal diseases. Lists of lawn diseases all cite watering too frequently as a contributing factor, and foliage leaf spot is promoted by repeated splashing of water onto leaves. Finally, watering landscapes too often is a waste of a very precious resource. Becoming more thoughtful about water usage will lead to healthier gardens and better conservation of Cape and Island resources.

When I speak to audiences about the importance of watering deeply but less often, people want me to give them hard and fast numbers for watering. Although I can recommend that in most cases landscapes get watered every week to ten days if it hasn't rained, it's impossible to give a length of time since every sprinkler or irrigation system is different, as is water pressure. The best I can say is to use a rain gauge set near your system, and measure how long it takes to fill the tube to between three quarters and one inch of water.

Moving into the future, water is likely to be a protected resource, so home landscapers must become more thoughtful about irrigation, plant selection, and placement. Plants that are drought tolerant will become more important to gardeners and landscapers. When designing new landscapes and refurbishing old ones, it's wise to group plants together according to their moisture needs. Place hydrangeas and roses, for example, in the same area since they need regular irrigation. But other beds can be filled with a selection of shrubs and perennials that tolerate dry soil. Such drought-tolerant plantings can be on a separate irrigation schedule.

LOCATION, LOCATION, LOCATION Realtors know that the three most important things about a property are all location, and gardeners soon learn this as well. In this region, proximity to the ocean not only determines real estate values, but also what grows well. Those who live closest

This tapestry of moss, lichens, bearberry, and mushrooms thrives in an area of pure sand in Wellfleet.

to the ocean, especially on the south-facing shores or in protected harbors, can often grow plants that would be marginally hardy in other locations. Yet in other areas, nearness to the ocean limits what can be grown. Drive from Woods Hole up to Provincetown and you'll notice that the trees get shorter and shorter. The combination of sand and wind on the outer Cape limit what will grow. Similarly, the vegetation on parts of Nantucket can be much shorter than that of most of Martha's Vineyard.

To be a gardener or home landscaper on the Cape and Islands means making peace with the soil and exposure to the weather. It requires us to work with what we've got, improving growing conditions the best we can and using a majority of plants that we know will thrive. It's also helpful to look at the micro-climates on every individual property; after observing windy or sheltered spots, making note of dry or wet areas, and learning about the native soil, the right plants can be chosen for each location.

CLIMATE CHANGE Given that the ocean already affects Cape and Islands' weather, what can we expect to see from the climate change that's happening worldwide? Current thinking is that weather events that have always been with us and vary from year to year may become more extreme. So we might experience stronger nor'easters or hurricanes, and longer periods of summer drought, for example. We have already seen that our normally warm falls are even milder, with later frosts, than in years past. This means more PJM Rhododendrons coming into partial flower in November and December instead of April, and green buds on our beloved *Hydrangea macrophylla* shrubs breaking dormancy at the same time.

Although we have no ability to modify a warming climate overnight, we can alter our garden and landscaping practices to accommodate such transformations. We can group plants according to their moisture needs

Pat McDonald, a volunteer master gardener and retired Barnstable elementary teacher of thirty years, created this peaceful oasis with strategically placed sitting areas for enjoying the gardens.

ABOVE: *This backyard shows what can be done with a variety of foliage colors and textures.* BELOW: *By artfully combining shrubs, trees and perennials, professional gardener Pamela Phipps has created a landscape where there is no lawn.*

so that in times of drought there are fewer areas to water. We can be sure to use a diverse selection of plants in our yards and gardens so that if some species die from drought or storms, there are others that will withstand those stresses. We can avoid planting monocultures such as long rows of one plant, for example. And as much as we love our signature plant, the blue hydrangea, we can be sure to include other shrubs in our landscapes that will flower even if rollercoaster temperatures might zap the buds on the mopheads.

In other words, we need to be flexible.

SUN & SHADE When growing plants we frequently see mentioned how much sun is required. "Full sun" and "full shade" are easy terms to understand. An area that is in full sun receives direct sunlight for at least seven or eight hours a day. An area that is in full shade gets no direct sun at all. It's

Joyce Jenks knows the wisdom of planting blue hydrangeas where they will be in part shade. If planted in full sun, the flowers on this type of Hydrangea will fade or brown quickly.

Plants can soften the edges of sheds or other outbuildings, turning a tool-storage area into what might be a cottage or guest house.

the "part sun" and "part shade" terminology that can be confusing.

"Part sun" is when an area is getting at least four hours of direct sun that includes the noon hour. So the parts of a landscape where the sun shines from ten to two, for example, or noon to four in the afternoon would qualify. "Part shade" is that same four hours of sun but on either end of the day. A corner of the garden that gets two hours of sun in the early morning and again in the late afternoon would be part shade. Some areas of a property might get some direct sun in the early morning or late in the day but during the rest of the time the sun is filtered through trees. That would also be part shade.

Most plants that grow best in full sun will be fine if they get four or five hours when the sun is the strongest, but when grown in shadier conditions they will flower less, stretch taller and grow thinner. These plants will flop or lean forward, reaching for the best light. All plants require less maintenance and are most attractive when they are grown in their preferred amount of sun or shade.

If you're looking for a plant to grow over small trellises, arbors or sheds in part shade, you can't go wrong with the Doyle's thornless blackberry. To maintain this plant it's necessary to cut the canes that bore fruit off in the fall, leaving the new stems that grew in the summer. These can be trained into place after the old ones are gone, and they will bear fruit the following season.

Plants For The Cape and Islands

IN THIS SECTION WE'LL CONSIDER great plants for this region. From annual flowering plants to lawns and trees, these chapters will cover those and others in between. Although the plants are generally grouped according to type, you'll notice that *Hydrangea* shrubs have their own chapter. *Hydrangeas* are so beloved in this region that it's the plant most people are

Endless Summer hydrangeas and yellow daylilies are a classic combination for Cape and Islands gardens. These thrive in Mairead Hinkey's and Robert Violetta's bayside gardens.

curious about. Beyond our favorite blue flowers, however, this section considers how to grow plants that bring joy to our hearts and gardens.

If I've missed your particular favorite variety or species, please forgive me, but I've limited these lists to plants that are most likely to thrive with minimal attention. There are many great selections that are often more difficult, marginally hardy, or considered "high maintenance." Some plants are prone to fungal problems from our cool, damp springs and others are likely to be damaged in high winds. In general I haven't included these in this book. The crape myrtle, for example, occasionally survives for several years in this area, but it's not a plant that is reliable. Marigolds thrive in hot summers but are prone to fungal leaf spot in wet seasons. These are just two examples of plants that haven't made the cut. That said I'm happy to share some of the plants that are especially suited to the region, along with general tips for growing them successfully.

This Harwich foundation planting is a celebration of summer with several hydrangeas, roses, Saint John's wort, yellow-foliage spireas, and perennial cat mint.

Chapter 3 *Annuals*

ANNUALS ARE PLANTS THAT don't live through the winter. Although these may be varieties that thrive from year to year in warmer areas, and some annuals self-seed in this region, for this book's purposes we're considering selections that die at the first hard frost.

Some people think that annuals are more work, but this is not true. Yes, you'll have to plant annuals every May, and unless you bring them indoors they will die in the fall. But most of these plants flower all summer and many of them require nothing but fertile soil to do so. And if you think that annuals are too expensive, I ask you to think about the last time you went out to dinner at a nice restaurant where you ordered drinks, a full

When planting Zinnias on the Cape and Islands, seeds can either be started inside in April or placed directly in the ground in early June. In either case, dust young seedlings with diatomaceous earth when they sprout or are placed in the ground to keep earwigs and slugs from stripping the tender leaves.

dinner, and maybe even wine or dessert. How much did you spend on that meal that lasted two to three hours? I suggest that for the same amount of money you can purchase many annuals that will bring you pleasure for four or more *months*.

SEEDS, SIX-PACKS OR POTS? Some annuals can be planted from seeds that are placed right in the ground in mid to late May. The only tricky part of growing annuals from seed in garden soil is distinguishing the annual seedlings from the weeds that will also be germinating at the same time. Inexperienced gardeners who will have trouble telling the difference will want to start their annual seeds in pots or flats, using seed-starting mix. Another trick is to plant your annual seeds in straight rows so it's easy to distinguish between your flowers and the weeds. Although weeds often seem devious, so far they haven't figured out how to grow in straight lines.

Janet Larsen Logan's front entry shows what power annuals have for delivering pops of color all summer. She's used four-inch pots of blue Scaevola, white Snow Princess Lobularia, pink New Guinea impatiens and purple Meteor Shower Verbena bonariensis from Proven Winners to provide flowers for before and after the daylilies bloom.

This annual planting is composed of plants purchased in six packs. 'Blue Horizon' Ageratum, African marigolds and Red Profusion Zinnia intermingle in a festival of primary colors. The Empress of India climbing Nasturtiums were grown from seed placed right into the ground.

Annuals that grow well from seed in the garden include alyssum (*Lobularia maritima*), nasturtium (*Tropaeolum majus*), California poppy (*Eschscholzia californica*) and zinnia (*Zinnia elegans*). The alyssum and poppies can be planted in early to mid May but the nasturtiums and zinnias should wait until the ground is warmer at the end of May. In cool, wet seasons, zinnia seeds could even be planted in the first week of June since they are prone to rotting in cold soil.

Commercially-grown annuals are available in either six-packs or pots. Six-pack plants are seed propagated, which is why they are less expensive. Most plants sold in pots are grown from cuttings, however, which is why they cost more. Many of the plants that are sold in small pots are never available in six packs.

FERTILIZING ANNUALS Annuals flower on new growth, so it's important that you stimulate that growth with regular fertilization. Although many fertilizers that contain high amounts of phosphorous are labeled as promoting flowers, this nutrient isn't that important for most annuals. Many of the newer varieties of annuals come from areas where there is little phosphorous in the soil, and these plants don't use phosphate-heavy fertilizers at all. The bottom line is that most annuals are nitrogen hogs, so look for fertilizers that are higher in nitrogen for these plants.

One method for easily fertilizing annuals is to use a combination of an organic fertilizer and a time-release synthetic. Use equal parts of these fertilizers, mixed before planting. The combination can be dug into the potting soil before you put plants in containers, or scattered over the ground before planting. The time-release synthetic starts feeding the plants immediately, and the organics kick in once those little pellets are almost finished. Using this method you won't have to mix up any liquids during the summer.

All the annuals at the front of this perennial garden were planted with an equal parts mix of time-release synthetic and granular organic fertilizer. That combination kept them nourished all summer and fall.

Annuals

ALL SUMMER ANNUALS There are annuals that bloom for a month or two and then stop flowering or die. Examples are blue *Lobelia*, corn poppies (*Papaver rhoeas*), bacopa (*Sutera* hybrids) and pansies (*Viola* hybrids). These are all early or cool-weather annuals that usually disappear once it gets hot. Some million bells (*Calibrachoa*) flower through the summer, while others slow or stop blooming when temperatures rise above the mid-seventies.

While these annuals flower early in the season, others such as morning glories (*Ipomoea sp.*) or dahlias (*Dahlia imperialis*) only begin to flower later in the summer. There are also annuals that flower best in specific conditions or with routine deadheading to remove the developing seeds. Vinca (*Catharanthus roseus*), marigolds (*Tagetes sp.*) and lantana (*Lantana camara*) flower best in hot, sunny weather, for example. These plants don't bloom as well in cool summers. Common geraniums (*Pelargonium* hybrids), most zinnias, *Angelonia*, and many petunias need constant deadheading or even pruning to keep them flowering. But there are other annuals that bloom all summer with little special attention, and these are what are listed here.

LOW-GROWING ANNUALS FOR THE CAPE & ISLANDS These plants generally stay under fourteen inches tall and can be used in the ground or in containers.

Axilflower (*Mecardonia* 'Gold Dust' or 'Gold Flake') Full to part sun.

Bidens (*Bidens ferulifolia* and others) Full to part sun.

Browallia (*Browallia speciosa*) Shade to part shade.

Cascading begonias (*Begonia boliviensis*) Shade to part shade.

Creeping zinnia (*Sanvitalia sp.* 'Starbini' or 'Sunbini') Sun.

'Diamond Frost' euphorbia (*Euphorbia hypericifolia* 'Inneuphe') Sun to part shade.

Evolvulus 'Blue My Mind' (*Evolvulus* hybrid 'USEVO1201') Sun.

Fan flower (*Scaevola aemula*) Sun to part sun.

New Guinea impatiens (*Impatiens hawkeri*) Sun to part shade.

Petunia (*Petunia* hybrids) Sun to part sun.

Profusion zinnias (*Zinnia x hybrida*) Sun to part sun.

Purslane (*Portulaca grandiflora*) Sun.

Rieger or Solenia begonias (*Begonia x hiemalis*) Sun to part shade.

'Snow Princess' alyssum (*Lobularia maritima* 'Snow Princess') Sun to part sun.

'SunPatiens' (*Impatiens hawkeri* 'Sunpatiens' series) Sun to part shade.

Wax begonias (*Begonia x Semperflorens-cultorum*) Sun to shade.

TALLER ANNUALS FOR THE CAPE & ISLANDS These plants grow well in the ground or in containers. Use these when you want flowers on taller stems.

'Blue Horizon' floss flower (*Ageratum houstonianum* 'Blue Horizon') Sun to part sun.

Cane begonias (*Begonia aconitifolia, B. coccinea* and crosses) Part sun to shade.

Cannas (*Canna indica*) Sun to part sun.

Dahlias (*Dahlia* hybrids) Sun to part sun.

'Fireworks' gomphrena (*Gomphrena globosa* 'Fireworks') Sun to part sun.

Flowering tobacco (*Nicotiana sylvestris* and *Nicotiana mutabilis*) Sun to part sun.

Salvia (*Salvia* hybrids) Sun to part sun.

'Señorita Rosalita' and 'Señorita Blanca' cleome (*Cleome* 'Inncleosr') Sun to part sun.

Tall Verbena (*Verbena bonariensis*) Sun to part sun.

Tropical hibiscus (*Hibiscus rosa-sinensis*) Sun to part sun.

ANNUALS WITH COLORFUL FOLIAGE Great annuals don't have to flower to bring color to the garden and containers. There are many lovely plants that add drama to your summer plantings with few or no blooms.

'Blazin' Lime' and 'Blazin' Rose' bloodleaf (*Iresine* hybrids) Part sun to shade.

Caladium (*Caladium bicolor*) Shade to part shade.

Coleus (*Solenostemon scutellarioides* and hybrids) Sun to shade.

'Little Ruby' Alternanthera (*Alternanthera dentate* 'Little Ruby') Sun to part sun.

Papyrus (*Cyperus papyrus* 'King Tut') Sun to part shade.

Persian shield (*Strobilanthes dyeriana*) Part sun to part shade.

Purple fountain grass (*Pennisetum setaceum rubrum*) Sun to part sun.

Purple heart (*Setcreasea pallida* or *Tradescantia pallida*) Sun.

Purple oxalis (*Oxalis triangularis*) Part sun to part shade.

Rex begonias (*Begonia rex-cultorum*) Part shade to shade.

'Silver Falls' dichondra (*Dichondra* 'Silver Falls') Sun to part shade.

Sweet potato vine (*Ipomoea* hybrids) Sun to part shade.

One of the best annual vines for flowering all summer are Mandevilla *hybrids. Be sure to read the tags carefully when you purchase plants, however, as there are some that stay short, and others, such as this Alice DuPont pink hybrid, that grow quite long.*

ANNUAL VINES   There are many lovely annual vines, but some grow better than others in this area. Smaller varieties such as cardinal climber (*Ipomoea sloteri*) and black-eyed Susan vine (*Thunbergia alata*) do well on small supports or hanging from baskets and sunny window boxes. The traditional blue morning glories (*Ipomoea indica*) grow large, but are famous for not flowering until fall. This is because they are triggered into bloom by decreasing hours of daylight. The most popular annual vines are *Mandevilla* hybrids and species. These are tropical plants and they flower all summer in part to full sun. They come in a variety of sizes, short to tall. Some don't need a trellis or other support and are good in hanging baskets, but others will climb a six to eight foot arbor in one season. Look for the type that suits the location where you will be growing the plants.

The plantings around one of John Sullivan's ponds combine shrubs, grasses, annuals, perennials and tropical plants to provide the most color and dramatic effects all summer.

ANNUALS PLANTING & CARE   With the exception of cool weather varieties such as pansies and *Osteospermum*, annuals are planted in late May on the Cape and Islands. Use the guideline of the night temperatures being reliably over fifty degrees Fahrenheit for timing.

If any annuals slow down in flower production during the summer, try cutting them in half and fertilizing with a synthetic liquid fertilizer. This is especially effective for petunias that grow long stems with flowers produced at the end of the stalks.

Water container annuals when they are dry. In hot weather, use this trick to be sure your pots are well hydrated: water all containers once, and then go back and fill them again. This double watering ensures that the entire

*In this front yard sitting area bold Canna leaves, African marigolds, coleus and
New Guinea impatiens are beautiful whether you're sitting on the front porch
or driving by on the street.*

root ball is soaked, because the first time water drains out in the gap between a root ball and the pot.

In-ground annuals, like most other plants, do well when watered deeply
every 6 to 10 days depending on the temperature. Although hand watering
can be sufficient for newly placed plants, it is seldom enough as the summer goes on. Unless local water restrictions dictate that plants be watered
by hand, a deep soaking with sprinklers or soaker hoses is far better. No
matter how you're delivering the moisture, when watering on hot summer
days, be sure to run the hose until the water comes out cool. If plants get hit
with water from a sun-heated hose, it can literally cook the foliage.

Remove annuals at the end of the season once they've been killed by hard
frost or are no longer an asset in the garden.

The pink petunias in this Nantucket windowbox echo the lovely pink hydrangeas. Along with the petunias are Snow Princess Lobularia, Diamond Frost Euphorbia, and Sky Blue Lobelia.

This brilliant use of annuals in the Rogers' garden in Brewster shows how to bring color to a shade garden. Baskets of Begonias and Impatiens were placed on plant stands so that they are above the greenery of the Hosta and ferns.

WINDOW BOXES & CONTAINERS   Small containers such as window boxes or pots under ten inches in diameter should be filled with fresh potting soil every spring. Over the course of the season roots fill these containers and nutrients are depleted. Better to put the old potting soil in the compost or vegetable garden and start out fresh if your containers are small. Do not put rocks or shards in the bottom of the pots, and make sure each container has at least one drainage hole.

Refresh large containers by removing the top twelve inches of potting medium, loosen what's left in the bottom and add a handful of a granular organic fertilizer. Then put new potting soil on the top and turn it into the bottom layer as best you can. Alternatively, all the soil can be removed from large pots and put in a garden cart or wheelbarrow. Use a shovel to break up the old roots, add some compost or fresh potting mix and a handful of granular, organic fertilizer. Mix it all well and then shovel the refreshed potting media back into the containers.

Since potting soils are usually an organically rich mix of peat moss, vermiculite and compost, often combined with bark and/or perlite, they grow heavier as the ingredients begin to break down. After four to five years of refreshing or top-dressing these older potting soils don't drain as well, and should be completely replaced.

OVER-WINTERING TENDER OR TROPICAL ANNUALS Commonly found annuals probably aren't worth trying to save from year to year. They are prone to insect infestations indoors, and will often become weak if they don't have enough light. But a few annuals are worth saving from year to year. Some, such as angel's trumpet (*Brugmansia*) and calla lilies (*Zantedeschia aethiopica*) can be put in a basement or other space where the temperature doesn't go much below forty degrees. Common geraniums (*Pelargonium* hybrids), tropical hibiscus (*Hibiscus rosa-sinensis*) and most succulents can be grown in a sunny window and most begonias will stay fairly attractive when grown as a houseplant in a bright window.

Plants that grow from tubers such as dahlias are easy to save. Clumps of tubers can be wrapped in layers of newspaper and stored in cardboard boxes in cool but not freezing locations. Separate individual tubers off the clumps in the spring for replanting.

Mandevilla are easy to overwinter inside, but most people find that the plants they save from year to year don't come into flower until late in the summer. If you want a plant that is in bloom from the beginning of June on, purchase a new plant that's been raised by a professional grower every year.

The beauty of herbs is that they can be grown in just about any sunny situation. Whether you create an arrangement of herbs in pots, place them in a dedicated herb garden, or mix them among shrubs or perennials, they are both ornamental and useful.

Chapter 4 *Herbs*

HERBS ARE ATTRACTIVE, useful and delicious plants that grow beautifully in full to part sun. These plants can be grown in separate herb gardens, among annuals and perennials and even in front of shrubs. All that's required to grow most herbs is well-drained soil and at least five hours of direct sun that includes the noon hour.

Herbs are more flavorful when kept on a lean diet. Less water and minimal nutrients create plants with greater aromatic oils, so a deep soaking once a week and little to no fertilizer is the best treatment. Perennial herbs also appreciate good winter drainage, so avoid planting them in low spots or places where water accumulates.

The most problematic herbs are those that spread prolifically. Most mints (*Mentha* sp.), lemon balm (*Melissa officinalis*), Russian comfrey (*Symphytum x uplandicum*) and oreganos (*Origanum* sp.) are called garden thugs because of their tendency to take over. These land-grabbers are best grown in

This variety of Italian basil called 'Amazel' is very late to flower and is resistant to basil downy mildew.

containers in most gardens. It's a mistake to include them in raised bed vegetable gardens unless you want to battle them forever.

BASIL (*Ocimum basilicum*) Annual. Plant in full sun once night temperatures are above fifty degrees Fahrenheit. [See 134 for information on Basil Downy Mildew]

CANNABIS (*C. indica*, *C. sativa* and hybrids) Annual. It is now legal for a resident in Massachusetts to grow six cannabis plants for his or her own use, provided those plants are out of sight and secure from the public. Grow this herb in very large containers (over 24" in diameter) or in the ground in full sun. Cannabis is triggered into flowering by equal hours of day and night, so outdoors it will begin to create buds in late August. Grow organically in well-drained soil, pinching the tips off of the young branches through mid-July to make bushier plants with more buds. Use synthetic fertilizers from the middle of summer on since organics take at least six weeks to become available to plants. Stop all applications of fertilizer at the end of August. Remember that first and foremost, this is a plant and the normal advice about growing plants applies. Unfortunately, there is far too much bad information and unnecessary product-driven advice on the Internet about growing this herb. Relax and remember how Mother Nature grows her plants, and you'll be fine with this one.

CHIVES (*Allium schoenoprasum*) Perennial for sun. Deadhead to avoid self-seeding.

CILANTRO (*Coriandrum sativum*) Annual. Sow seeds every three to four weeks in full sun for a continual supply of fresh coriander greens all summer and fall.

DILL (*Anethum graveolens*) Annual. Plant seeds every three weeks in full sun for continual harvest of dill greens.

FRENCH TARRAGON (*Artemisia dracunculus* var. *sativa*) Perennial. When shopping for tarragon plant, pinch off a leaf and test for fragrance and flavor. While French tarragon has both, Russian tarragon has neither and occasionally these plants can be mislabeled. When planting new, tender plants, wait until late May or early June in this region since young greenhouse-grown plants can succumb to the cold when placed outdoors too early.

LAVENDER (*Lavandula angustifolia* 'Phenomenal' and 'Munstead') Perennial. Lavender is a traditional component of herb and perennial gardens.

Although there are several species and cultivars, these two are the hardiest for Cape gardens. Lavender loves good drainage, full sun and a neutral pH soil. It also does best when planted near rocks or other heat-reflecting surfaces. Prune lavender every spring once new growth appears, removing all dead stems and trimming live ones back by about two inches. Shearing these plants once flowers fade also encourages full, bushy growth and some repeat flowering.

LEMON VERBENA (*Aloysia citrodora*) Annual. Sun or part sun.

PARSLEY (*Petroselinum crispum*) Biennial that bolts early in its second year. Plant every spring in full to part sun.

PINEAPPLE SAGE (*Salvia elegans*) Annual. This large-growing salvia is a good nectar source for late-migrating hummingbirds. Look for the variety called 'Golden Delicious' because its brilliant yellow foliage will be attractive all summer before the red flowers form in the fall.

ROSEMARY (*Rosmarinus officinalis*) Annual to tender perennial. The variety called 'Salem' is more tolerant of the low light indoors, but pay attention to the watering. Although rosemary is a very drought-tolerant plant when grown outdoors, it dries out quickly inside. Herb lovers are fond of saying that "when grown in a pot, a dry rosemary is a dead rosemary."

SAGE (*Salvia officinalis*) Perennial. Full sun and good drainage are required for this herb.

THYME (*Thymus vulgaris* and other species) Perennial. Cooks will want to plant the common thyme and lemon thyme (*T. citriodorus*) while those looking for attractive groundcovers in sunny areas will appreciate wooly thyme (*T. pseudolanuginosus*), creeping thyme (*Thymus serpyllum*), white thyme (*Thymus praecox* 'Albiflorus'), and Doretta Klaber thyme (*Thymus praecox* 'Doretta Klaber').

WALKING ONIONS (*Allium x wakegi*) This variety of allium is named for the way it "walks" around a garden. The plant forms small bulbils or bulblets, on top of stems, and as these grow larger and heavier they bend to the soil, planting themselves in a nearby location. Most people get this plant from another gardener or a plant sale as it's seldom sold in stores. The greens can be used as scallions in cooking, and it's a visually amusing plant in the garden as well.

TOP LEFT: *Now that growing a few plants is legal in Massachusetts, Cannabis is being cultivated for a variety of recreational and medicinal reasons. Strains that are higher in CBD rather than THC are especially of interest to those who wish to use the plant for conditions such as insomnia or arthritis.*
TOP RIGHT: *Lemon Verbena should be grown in a pot on every patio or deck for aromatherapy alone. It's useful for making teas, as flavoring for cocktails, or to place in bouquets for fragrance, and a small plant will quadruple its size in a single summer.* **BOTTOM LEFT:** *Laura Urban's garden in Harwich makes good use of the drought-tolerant perennial Santolina. Although this is often planted in herb gardens, Santolina isn't used for culinary purposes, but on slopes that are hard to water it's the perfect plant. Here it's nicely combined with orange flowering butterfly weed (*Asclepias tuberosa*).*
BOTTOM RIGHT: *Don and Phyllis Helfrich planted purple coneflower (*Echinacea purpurea*), red bee balm (*Monarda didyma*), white Shasta daisies (*Leucanthemum x superbum*), and black-eyed Susans (*Rudbeckia hybrid*) for a mid-summer show of flowers in their backyard.*

Chapter 5 *Perennials*

I OFTEN COMPARE HAVING a perennial garden to being a fourth grade teacher. These educators are challenged by rooms filled with students with a wide range of experiences and abilities. One child sits still for hours on end and another cannot. Some are visual learners and others learn by hearing the information. One child has had breakfast and another comes to school with low blood sugar. The teacher needs to figure out what each child needs to be able to learn well, while still keeping order in the classroom.

A perennial garden is like that schoolroom. One plant needs to be divided frequently to do well while another can be left in place for years. Some plants need very fertile soil while others bloom better in lean conditions. One needs to be staked while another is sturdy. Some need full sun and others part shade. And we gardeners need to learn what each plant needs and still keep order in the garden.

This analogy helps people to understand that although these plants come up every year (usually) a perennial garden is the most high maintenance garden you can plant. Because every plant has different requirements for growing well, the perennial gardener needs to be in this garden more often. Perennials need to be weeded, divided, mulched and deadheaded frequently. And since weeds sneakily get established in and under perennials, and they sprout and grow twelve months a year, the necessity for weeding is constant.

Although the reality is that most perennial garden maintenance can be done just about anytime, here is a general guide to the tasks necessary to keep such a garden looking its best.

SPRING: Clear out fallen leaves; cut winter-browned foliage off plants; divide plants that have stopped flowering well, have grown into a donut-shaped clump, or have died out in the center; edit out overly enthusiastic spreaders so they don't take over the garden; fertilize with a granular, organic fertilizer if a soil test indicates it's needed; top dress established beds with an inch of compost or composted manure; mulch soil between plants with an inch or two of mulch, keeping it away from the crowns of the plants; cut a few inches off woody plants such as lavender and Russian sage; pull weeds, especially those that sprouted and grew in the winter such as chickweed, the various cresses and the low-growing *Veronica repens.*

SUMMER: Water deeply once a week if nature hasn't supplied an inch of rain in ten days or longer; pull weeds regularly; remove spent flowers and stems that are no longer attractive on iris, peonies, daylilies, and early-flowering salvias.

FALL: Divide and transplant as needed, but don't do this after the end of September; pull weeds as they appear; cut down any perennials that have wilted or browned after frost, but leave those with leaves that still look capable of photosynthesis.

WINTER: Mulch tender perennials with salt-marsh hay or pine boughs in late December; pull weeds when the ground isn't frozen. Note that most perennials that are winter-hardy on the Cape and Islands do not need any mulch for winter protection.

PERENNIAL DETAILS

Some perennials that flower in the early summer such as catmint (*Nepeta*), beardtongue (*Penstemon*), spiderwort (*Tradescantia*) and perennial salvia (*Salvia*) aren't garden assets after they flower. These plants can all be cut to the ground after flowering and they will grow new, fresh foliage. Do this around the Fourth of July.

Treat Montauk daisies as if they are small shrubs. Trim off dead stem tops in early spring, and prune off any branches that are lying flat on the ground. You can shear these back by a couple inches in early June if you want, but never after June 10th. Montauk daisies can be cut to six inches above the ground in the spring, but those new stems are more likely to flop.

Another group of plants prone to flopping are the tall sedums. Keep these perennials on a lean diet with little water and fertilizer. Growing 'Autumn Joy' and other taller sedum in rich soil or moist conditions will cause the stems to open and fall by late summer.

Note that the green and white variegated varieties of *Hosta* are often chewed up by August since earwigs and slugs find the white parts irresistible. Also, *Hosta* are prone to unsightly leaf-spot fungus if they are hit with irrigation on a frequent basis. Remove the flower stems once the blooms fade.

If a peony is grown in full sun it can remain untouched for decades, but once the foliage starts to brown or get powdery mildew in late August, cut the plant to the ground. Plant so the top of the root is only two inches under the soil's surface. Peonies will stop flowering if the area where they are growing has gotten progressively shadier.

Perennial geraniums that are looking leggy can be cut to the ground in mid-summer. Rozanne and the *sanguineum* varieties respond to this haircut very well and return with new foliage and flowers.

LOW-MAINTENANCE PERENNIAL PLANTS Although there are many lovely perennials that are hardy on the Cape and Islands, this list focuses on plants that are reliable and relatively low-maintenance. I have not included

In June the peonies (Paeonia *hybrids*) *are the star of the show with Serbian bell-flower* (Campanula poscharskyana) *and 'Southern Comfort' Heuchera planted in front and Black Lace Sambucus flowers in the back of this bed at the same time.*

In July this same flowerbed is still enhanced by the 'Southern Comfort' Heu-chera, now grown larger, along with the graceful Aureola hakone grass (Ha-konechloa macra 'Aureola'). The peonies have been deadheaded so the foliage looks good. In the background there are spires of Verbascum chaixii; *these will get cut down to the ground as soon as they finish flowering. This bed is a good example of how keeping a perennial garden looking good takes ongoing work.*

plants that spread quickly, need frequent dividing, or are short-lived since these require more constant attention.

PERENNIAL BULBS

I'm going to include bulbs in with the perennial section because most people want the spring-flowering bulbs they plant to come back every year. There are two problems with this expectation. The first is that some bulbs, notably tulips, can be short-lived. Plant them only three inches deep and cover with two inches of mulch to help them return for at least three years.

The second problem in this region is that in many places the soil is just too sandy to support bulb health and good spring flower return, even of the more reliable bulbs such as daffodils. For the best spring flower display, plant bulbs in well-amended soils, not in pure sand, and fertilize sandy soils in early spring just before flowering. Leave bulb foliage in the garden until it falls and turns yellow; do not cut it off or tie, knot and braid it.

That said, the following bulbs perform well when planted in full to part sun on the Cape and Islands.

ALLIUM (*Allium* species and varieties) The smaller varieties are longer lasting. Part sun/full sun.

CAMASSIA (*Camassia leichtlinii*) Blue flower spikes grow to about three feet tall. Camassia is also one of the few bulbs that tolerate wet soils in winter. Part sun/full sun.

CROCUS (*Crocus vernus*) Plant in flower beds or naturalize in lawns. Part shade/full sun.

DAFFODIL (*Narcissus* species and varieties) Varieties commonly planted for naturalizing, as are Ice Follies, Cheerfulness, Mount Hood, and the poet's daffodil, *Narcissus poeticus recurvus*. No matter what variety you plant, you don't have to deadhead these plants. It's a myth that you have to cut the seeds off the stems to keep strength in the bulbs; leave the plants alone until the stems and leaves turn yellow. You can also ignore daffodil shoots that poke up in the fall or mid-winter. These autumnal sprouts are normal and don't need to be covered or otherwise protected from the cold. Part shade/full sun.

GRAPE HYACINTHS (*Muscari armeniacum*) These bulbs naturally send foliage up in the fall. Grape hyacinths self-seed and will naturalize in lawns and gardens. Part shade/full sun.

HYACINTHS (*Hyacinthus orientalis*) For the best fragrant hyacinths display, feed these bulbs with a liquid fertilizer as the flowers fade. If you've purchased potted hyacinths in the spring, plant them four to six inches deep after the flowers fade and fertilize at that time. Full sun.

One of the largest collections of snowdrops (Galanthus sp.) can be found in Jonathan and Eugenie Shaw's garden in Sandwich. They have many species and varieties of these bulbs that flower in late winter into early spring. Since snowdrops disappear later in the summer, they can be grown in shade gardens, lawns or under shrubs.

This summer phlox (Phlox paniculata 'Jeana') is especially resistant to mildew. Since the flowers are slightly smaller than others in the same species it is also a great flower for cutting.

LEFT: *Camassia* (Camassia leichtlinii caerulea) *might be native to the Pacific Northwest, but it grows very well in Massachusetts. Plant this bulb in between later-flowering perennial hibiscus, since the camassia foliage goes dormant by July.*
RIGHT: *Hyacinth flowers look especially good when grouped closely together.*

SIBERIAN SQUILL (*Scilla siberica*) With grass-like leaves and bright blue flowers, *Scilla* is another favorite for naturalizing or under-planting perennials and shrubs. Part shade/full sun.

SNOWDROPS (*Galanthus nivalis*) These elegant flowers appear in February and March. Snowdrops will spread and grow in part sun to lightly shaded areas. Part shade/full sun.

WOOD HYACINTHS (*Hyacinthoides hispanica*) Twelve to fifteen inch flower spikes in blue, pink or white flowers appear in late May to early June. Because their foliage goes dormant by July, they are perfect to plant in between perennials that flower later in the summer. If left to go to seed these will politely sow themselves around a garden. Part shade/full sun.

Reliable Perennials for the Cape & Islands

Balloon flower (*Platycodon grandiflorus* hybrids) Sun to part sun.

Barrenwort (*Epimedium* species and hybrids) Shade to part shade.

Big root geranium (*Geranium macrorrhizum*) Part sun to part shade.

Bleeding heart (*Dicentra spectabilis* and *eximia*) Part sun to shade.

Bush clover (*Lespedeza thunbergii*) Sun to part sun.

Cat mint (*Nepeta faassenii* 'Walker's Low' and other varieties) Sun to part sun.

Coral bells (*Heuchera* hybrids) Part sun to shade.

Creeping phlox (*Phlox subulata*) Sun and good drainage.

Creeping soapwort (*Saponaria officinalis*) Sun and good drainage.

Daylily (*Hemerocallis* species and hybrids) Sun to part sun.

Dwarf liatris (*Liatris microcephala*) Sun to part sun.

Eastern blue star (*Amsonia hubriechtii* and *A. tabernaemontana*) Sun to part sun.

False indigo (*Baptisia australis*) Sun to part sun.

False sunflower (*Heliopsis helianthoides* 'Prairie Sunset') Sun to part sun.

Foam flower (*Tiarella cordifolia* cultivars including 'Spring Symphony') Shade to part shade.

Giant fleece flower (*Persicaria polymorpha*) Sun.

Hardy hibiscus aka rose mallow (*Hibiscus moscheutos*) Sun to part sun.

Hellebores aka Christmas rose and Lenten rose (*Helleborus niger* and *H. orientalis*) Part shade to shade.

Hosta (*Hosta* hybrids) Part sun to shade.

'Iron Butterfly' vernonia (*Vernonia lettermannii* 'Iron Butterfly') Sun to part sun.

Japanese forest grass or hakone grass (*Hakonechloa macra* 'Aureola' and 'All Gold') Part sun to shade.

Japanese painted fern (*Athyrium niponicum* 'Pictum') Shade to part shade.

Lady fern (*Athyrium filix-femina*) Shade to part shade.

Lesser calamint (*Calamintha nepeta* ssp. Nepetoides) Great pollinator plant. Sun to part sun.

Montauk daisy, aka Nippon daisy (*Nipponanthemum nipponicum*) Sun.

Moonshine yarrow (*Achillea* 'Moonshine') Sun.

Peony (*Paeonia lactiflora* hybrids and tree peonies, *Paeonia suffruticosa*) Sun.

Perennial geranium (*Geranium* 'Rozanne' and *sanguineum*) Sun to part shade.

Perennial mums, aka Korean mums (*Dendranthema* 'Sheffield Pink' 'Cambodian Queen' 'Autumn Moon') Sun to part sun.

Purple bugbane (*Actaea simplex* 'Brunette' and other dark cultivars, aka *Cimicifuga*) Part sun to shade.

Purple coneflower (*Echinacea purpurea* and cultivars. 'Milkshake' is especially nice.) Sun.

Russian sage (*Perovskia atriplicifolia*) Sun.

Sedge (*Carex morrowii* 'Silk Tassel' and *oshimensis* 'Evergold') Part sun to shade.

Sedum 'Autumn Joy' 'Pure Joy' & 'Autumn Charm' (*Sedum* hybrids) Sun.

Stokes aster (*Stokesia laevis*) Sun.

Summer phlox (*Phlox paniculata* 'David' (white), 'Lavender David' (pinky purple) and 'Jeana' (pink) are all mildew resistant. 'Volcano Purple' and the rest in the 'Volcano' series are repeat flowering.) Sun.

Yellow wax bells (*Kirengeshoma palmatae*) Shade to part shade.

Chapter 6
Ornamental Grasses

THERE ARE MANY TYPES OF GRASSES, from those we use to grow a lawn, to the American beach grass on our dunes, and on to the ornamental grasses we plant in landscapes and gardens. Some plants that we think of as grass, like the native *Carex pensylvanica* that grows in the dappled shade of our woodlands, isn't a grass at all, but a sedge. For homeowners, what's important is finding the right plant for their landscapes.

Many people call all ornamental grasses "beach grass" but it's important to learn the difference between the true beach grass, *Ammophila breviligulata*, which grows on our dunes and other landscape plants. The native American beach grass spreads and is one of the few plants that will tolerate growing in pure sand, salt spray and in near-constant winds. It grows to about two feet tall, helps stabilize sand dunes, and will mingle with other plants that also tolerate such harsh conditions.

As valuable and attractive as this grass is, it's not usually what people want in smaller yards and gardens. Better to learn to refer to our landscape grasses as "ornamental grass" and to be clear about selecting a plant that will do well in the growing conditions you have. Most ornamental grasses that people see on the Cape and Islands do best in full sun.

Most ornamental grasses grow quite large. The most popular ones in this region are in the genus *Miscanthus*, and these grow between six to eight feet in diameter quite quickly. Many a homeowner has planted their ornamental grasses too close together only to find that they are less attractive when crowded, and are difficult to transplant or divide once they've grown so large. A general rule of thumb is to space all *Miscanthus* varieties at least eight feet apart, measured center-to-center.

Secondly, most grasses are at their peak from August through October. So although they can be quite tall during this period, they are not good screening plants the rest of the year. And finally, many grasses are prone to rust disease when they are hit frequently with irrigation; water these plants for a longer period of time but only once a week.

Because grasses are attractive through the early winter, it's common to wait and cut them down after Thanksgiving or as part of a spring cleanup. Don't wait too long, however, because in April the new foliage will start to push up and clipping that off along with the old will make your plants less attractive as they grow.

Since many people feel that grasses give a landscape a beachy look that's appropriate to this region, I've included a description of the grasses listed here. Choose a grass that will fit in the space available so that you won't be fighting it later; many are difficult to move or divide once they are over three years old.

FEATHER REED GRASS (*Calamagrostis* x *acutiflora* 'Karl Foerster') If you want an upright grass that doesn't grow too wide, this is a good choice.

Given the sand that surrounds this house near the ocean in Truro, Scott Warner and David Kirchner made a wise decision to plant part of their property with the true American beach grass (Ammophila breviligulata). *In this location this plant not only grows where few other plants would thrive, but it adds to the sense of place in the overall garden design.*

It doesn't have the white plumes in the fall that we often associate with ornamental grasses, and the plants grow between four and five feet high. *Calamagrostis* is good for smaller spaces, or to plant in a swath that won't end up forming an oppressive wall. Sun to part sun.

FOUNTAIN GRASS (*Pennisetum alopecuroides* 'Hameln') Fountain grass forms a round clump and has foxtail-type flowers in the fall. The straight species grows four feet tall and up to six feet wide, but the variety 'Hameln' is the most commonly used *Pennisetum* on the Cape and Islands. Other varieties with pinkish plumes are 'Moudry,' 'Desert Plains' and 'Red Head' but these self-seed fairly vigorously and usually need to be deadheaded so that your driveway, lawn and other gardens don't become fountain grass breeding grounds. Sun to part sun.

JAPANESE FOREST GRASS (*Hakonechloa macra* 'Aureola' and 'All Gold') These two yellow-foliaged grasses grow to about two feet tall and are the best grasses for part shade. Part sun to part shade.

SILVER GRASS (*Miscanthus sinensis* varieties) Silver grass, aka Japanese silver grass, is the most widely planted ornamental grass on the Cape and Islands. There are several cultivars, from the white striped 'Variegatus' to the very tall porcupine grass (M. s. 'Strictus'). Best suited for smaller yards and gardens are 'Morning Light,' 'Adagio' or 'Yaku Jima.' Be aware that even the short varieties reach six feet plus in diameter. In many areas *Miscanthus* grasses are proving to be invasive. So far this is not the case on the Cape and Islands, but those who want to avoid plants that self-seed might want to choose a different variety. Sun to part sun.

SWITCHGRASS (*Panicum virgatum*) In the wild our native switchgrass provides nesting cover for birds and seeds for an assortment of wildlife. In the garden this plant grows between three and five feet tall and is very soft in appearance. There are a few varieties available with bluish foliage, and one, 'Ruby Ribbons,' turns burgundy as the weather cools. *Panicum* is occasionally seeded or plug-planted on slopes for soil stabilization or as a tall ground cover. Sun to part sun.

OTHER GRASSES, RUSHES & SEDGES

Gardeners and students of horticulture have a saying that helps them distinguish grasses from reeds and sedge plants. "Sedges have edges; rushes are round; grasses are hollow right up from the ground." In general, the foliage on sedges is triangular and so has edges, rushes are completely round and grasses are hollow. There are a few rushes and sedges that are available for home landscapes.

COMMON RUSH (*Juncus effusus*) This native rush frequently grows near kettle ponds or in wetlands. There are cultivated varieties as well, most grow between a foot to three feet tall depending on the moisture available. These can self-seed, so pull them out if they spread where you don't want rushes to grow, and cut them down in the spring to refurbish the look of the plants. Sun to part shade.

PENNSYLVANIA SEDGE (*Carex pensylvanica*) This shade-loving grass is native to our dry woodlands on the Cape and Islands. It is semi-evergreen and never needs mowing, but the clumping habit means that it's not really suitable as a lawn substitute except in plantings where there is little foot traffic. Part sun to part shade.

PURPLE LOVE GRASS (*Eragrostis spectabilis*) This low-growing grass looks best planted in large groups and it thrives in poor, well-drained soils. It grows one to two feet tall and is well suited to meadows or other casual, native plantings. This grass is not commonly available in nurseries but is sold in bulk in plug form from growers found online. Sun.

SILK TASSEL SEDGE (*Carex morrowii* 'Silk Tassel') Although this sedge is not frequently found in garden centers, I predict that it will soon become more popular as a shade grass. The blades are thin and light in color, and the plants stay in neat, round tufts that are about six inches tall. Their texture and size make them the perfect plant to use near any *Hosta*. Part sun to part shade.

YELLOW SEDGES (*Carex oshimensis* varieties such as 'Evergold,' 'Everillo,' 'Everest,' 'Everoro') This series of sedge plants comes in a variety of yellow-foliaged selections. These grow well in part sun to part shade and often look good through the winter. Cut them back to near the ground in March or early April to refresh winter-worn leaves. The blooms on these plants aren't very attractive, and usually appear in the spring. Clip them off as desired, or wait until blooms appear in the spring to shear the plants down to renew the foliage. Part sun to part shade.

One of the best groundcovers for shade and part shade is Epimedium. *Because it grows so thickly, weeds aren't able to grow in the area once this perennial is established. Some varieties spread more quickly than others.* Epimedium sulphureum *is an especially vigorous variety.*

Chapter 7 *Groundcovers*

THE PURPOSE OF A GROUNDCOVER is, of course to fill an area and conceal the soil. Since Mother Nature seems to dislike bare dirt, she will always plant weeds in any open areas. Groundcovers are a gardener's way of filling spaces before Nature has other ideas about what should be growing there. A good groundcover spreads but not invasively, and grows thickly enough to outcompete the weeds.

Although some prefer their groundcovers to be low-growing and evergreen, their height and visibility through the winter are probably less important than their weed-smothering abilities. But in their quest to have it all, many make the mistake of choosing plants that either don't perform as needed or grow so well that they become long-term problem plants.

At this writing English and Baltic ivy (*Hedera helix* and *H. helix* 'Baltica') aren't on Massachusetts's invasive plant lists, but nevertheless, they are aggressive, problematic plants. Ivy not only outcompetes the weeds, it takes over lawns, climbs up trees and destroys native plants. Many homeowners find that the ivy planted as an evergreen groundcover thirty or forty years ago is now systematically taking over their entire yard.

If you are looking for groundcovers, do not consider ivy. And if you need to get rid of the plants that are currently on your property or invading from your neighbor's land, get a professional landscaper to help.

Two other disappointing groundcovers are periwinkle (*Vinca minor*) and 'Blue Rug' junipers. These plants aren't so aggressive, although in the right circumstances *Vinca* can spread out of bounds. No, these groundcovers are frustrating because they don't outcompete the weeds. Neither plant is thick enough to prevent weeds from popping up in and among its branches, and once grass or other weeds get established among *Vinca* or junipers, it's impossible to remove. Instead of a neat, low-maintenance landscape you end up with a mess of untidy weeds.

Unlike periwinkle and the 'Blue Rug' juniper, the following plants *are* good for weed suppression. Planting guidelines that are given for spacing plants are for those who want an area to be completely covered in about five years. If you're in a hurry, plant them six to twelve inches closer together.

BARRENWORT (*Epimedium sulphureum*) This variety of *Epimedium* spreads enough to be considered a weed-suppressing groundcover and tolerates dry shade. Plant three feet apart in part to full shade.

BIG ROOT GERANIUM (*Geranium macrorrhizum*) This is one of my favorite workhorse perennials. Weed-smothering, deer or rabbit resistant, and attractive. Space these plants two to three feet apart in part sun to part shade.

CAREX 'ICE DANCE' (*Carex morrowii* 'Ice Dance') Since 'Ice Dance' spreads fairly quickly, place plants three to five feet apart. This is a semi-evergreen, grass-like sedge for people who want to cover larger areas of ground. 'Ice Dance' grows to about a foot tall. Shade to part shade.

GREEN AND GOLD (*Crysogonum virginianum* 'Allen Bush') A native groundcover, this low-growing variety of *Crysogonum* tolerates flooding and drought. Bright yellow flowers will cover dark green plants in May and appear sporadically during the summer. Plant three to four feet apart in part sun to part shade.

GREEN MOUND JUNIPER (*Juniperus procumbens* 'Green Mound') Unlike others in the same genus, this low juniper grows so tightly that most weeds can't get established. Junipers do best in well-drained soils that aren't frequently hit with irrigation although a weekly watering will be needed while the plants are getting established. Full to part sun.

HOSTA (*Hosta* varieties) Although most hosta doesn't spread quickly, they so totally shade the ground weeds can't get established. There are thousand of *Hosta* varieties but 'Lemon Lime,' 'June,' and 'Blue Cadet' are quite vigorous and don't grow above fifteen inches. Shade to part shade.

LADY'S MANTLE (*Alchemilla mollis*) This plant self-seeds rather than spreads via roots and rhizomes, so it's suitable only for areas where you'll be happy with Mother Nature doing the plant placement. That said, it's especially attractive on either side of stone steps in a shade garden. The foliage tends to brown out in the summer when planted in hot afternoon sun. Part sun to shade.

PACHYSANDRA (*Pachysandra terminalis*) Also called Japanese spurge, this is a "be careful what you wish for" plant. Yes, it grows in shade, is weed-smothering and is evergreen. But where it's happy it will fill entire beds and choke out all but the larger shrubs or established hosta. Shade to part shade.

ZAGREB COREOPSIS (*Coreopsis* 'Zagreb') Although this coreopsis is taller than most groundcover plants, it's one of the best for spreading quickly in sunny, dry locations. The small yellow flowers are cheerful in mid-summer and the black seed heads that form in late summer are equally attractive. Sun to part sun.

Lady's mantle (Alchemilla mollis) *makes a pleasing groundcover in part shade. Although this plant looks better if it's deadheaded after the flowers fade, leaving a few to go to seed will help the plant spread.*

Chapter 8
Vegetables & Fruit

THE CAPE AND ISLANDS is a wonderful region for growing edibles. Those who raise fruits and vegetables know that their efforts are rewarded by most flavorful food on earth. Like in other categories of plants, some varieties do better than others. In general, for example, strawberries, blueberries and raspberries do better than fruit trees. Yes, you can grow apples, plums, cherries and peaches, but because there are several diseases that are problematic for those plants, they don't always thrive. Pear trees fare a bit better.

In addition to diseases, home fruit growers need to fend off birds and

When the author goes into her vegetable garden in August and asks, "What's for dinner?" the answer is usually the contents of this basket. Broccoli, Tuscan kale, tomatoes, Costata Romanesco and Zephyr summer squash, and Black Beauty eggplant.

small critters such as chipmunks as their fruit ripens. Unless you have acres of fruiting bushes, if you want much fruit it's likely that you'll need to net the plants. Those who have enough space often grow blueberries in a cage covered with hardware cloth or a similar wire fencing that small birds can't squeeze through. (More in Chapter 16: *Animals*)

Vegetables tend to be a bit easier to grow, but in the veggie garden there are also problems that gardeners dance with. From early blight on tomatoes to powdery mildew on squash; from the holes that cabbage looper larvae create on broccoli to the basil downy mildew that causes our favorite herb to yellow and die, the edible garden is filled with potential problems. However viewing these challenges as dancing partners, rather than adversaries, can help the home gardener maintain a positive perspective while growing large harvests despite the trials.

Fruit That Grows Well on The Cape & Islands

Blackberries (*Rubus* species) Since most blackberries are very thorny, managing a blackberry patch can be difficult, not to mention painful. Look for varieties such as 'Triple Crown' or 'Doyle's,' which are thornless and grow large berries. These plants are perfect for growing on arbors and trellises. Part shade/sun.

Blueberries (*Vaccinium corymbosum*) Highbush blueberries are probably the most successfully grown fruit in this region provided you net or cage them to keep the birds away. There are varieties that flower early, mid-season and later, and with several of each you can pick berries from the Fourth of July into September. Be sure to plant at least two of each variety, however, for good pollination. Have a soil test done to test for pH since these plants need acidic soil that tests between 4.5 and 5.5.

Blueberries also bear best when one or more of the oldest canes are cut down to a foot tall or shorter every spring, and crossed branches are removed on top. This stimulates new growth and better production of berries. Spray spinosad for winter moth larvae when they hatch in late March or early April, and again on the emerging foliage in May as long as bees aren't foraging. Spray again as berries form in July to help control the spotted wing fruit fly (*Drosophila suzukii*). To prevent fruit from spoiling quickly from this fruit fly, eat or freeze berries as they become ripe. Part sun/sun.

You'll have a bigger crop of berries if you plant several shrubs in a few varieties. Hybrids that grow and bear well in this area include Duke, Patriot (both early), Blueray, Bluecrop (mid-season), Chandler, Darrow (late mid-season) and Jersey (late).

RASPBERRIES (*Rubus idaeus* and other species) These plants need to be well tended or they will become a low-fruiting briar patch instead of a raspberry bed. At the end of the summer cut all canes that bore fruit to the ground. Leave those that haven't produced fruit yet but clip the tops or cut to about four feet tall to encourage branching. Remove dead canes as they appear, and dig out plants that spread into pathways and other gardens. Mulch to control weeds. Part shade/sun.

RHUBARB (*Rheum rhabarbarum*) If there was ever a trouble-free edible, rhubarb is that plant. Only the stalks (aka leaf petioles) are edible, and these are best harvested in May or early June. Mulch to control weeds, and fertilize with an organic fertilizer if you have sandy soils. Part shade/sun.

STRAWBERRIES (*Fragaria x ananassa*) Like raspberries, strawberries need regular tending in order to be most productive. Offshoots need to be dug and replanted in rows once they have rooted near the mother plant, and older plants removed after two years. When planted in rows it is easier to keep track of the age of the plants, and somewhat easier to protect the fruit from chipmunks and other critters. Part sun/sun.

VEGETABLES

Vegetables can be grown in the ground, in containers or in raised beds. If you are new to vegetable gardening I suggest you start by growing some things in pots and others in turned soil at ground level. Even if you plan to build raised beds later, planting in the soil for the first season or two will help prepare the area well and should you not like veggie gardening as much as you originally thought you would, you can easily turn that area back to lawn. Once raised vegetable beds are constructed it's more difficult to make them look like anything else.

VEGETABLE GARDEN SUCCESS

☙ Pick the sunniest place you have. Vegetables need at least six hours of dead-on sun including the noon hour. Take soil samples for a soil test to see if you need to fertilize or lime; never assume that you need either or both.

☙ Loosen the soil well. Spread a three or four-inch layer of compost or composted manure on the surface and then dig or till it into the ground. Smooth the soil with a rake.

☙ If you plan on making raised beds in the future, create in-ground beds that are about four feet deep and eight feet long. These measurements work well with standard lengths of lumber, and it's easy to tend the area without walking on the soil. When soil is loose the vegetables grow more quickly.

☙ After planting, mulch with organic material such as hay, chopped leaves or seaweed. This keeps weeds down, helps the soil to stay moist and adds organic matter that improves the soil for the future.

☙ Whenever possible, water vegetables deeply but less often using soaker hoses or sprinklers. Hand-watering with a hose is seldom deep enough unless you're watering seedlings or newly-placed plants.

☙ When growing in containers, make them large. Unless you're just growing a decorative pot, containers should be at least two feet in diameter or larger. You can grow vegetables in wood, metal, plastic, fiberglass or fabric pots, as long as the container has drainage holes.

☙ Fill containers completely with a mix of bagged topsoil and potting soil. Use one part topsoil mixed with two parts potting mix. Do not put rocks, shards, mulch or other materials in the bottom of the pot.

☙ In the spring or fall, add compost or aged manure to beds. To refresh containers, dump the old soil in a bin or wheelbarrow, chop up the old roots and turn in some compost and a granular organic fertilizer. Fill your containers with that restored, freshened mix.

Till or No-Till?

In the past few years there has been a great deal written about no-till vegetable gardening. In truth, there are advantages to turning the soil and there are benefits with the zero-tillage method as well. Here are the pros and cons for each approach, so you can make your own decision about the technique that will work best for you.

In a no-till garden the soil is turned initially, and amendments added before your first crops are planted, but the soil is seldom turned after that. Mulch is kept on the surface and this amends from the top down. Not turning the soil is less work because you keep the mulch in place and you aren't exposing new weed seeds to the light. Additionally, the natural soil structure created by the plants, beneficial fungi, and other microorganisms isn't disturbed.

Some who use the no-till method keep a layer of mulch about six inches thick on the bed at all times, and tuck their compostable kitchen garbage (eggshells, coffee grounds, vegetable scraps, etc.) under the mulch to compost right in the garden. As the mulch and scraps decompose, more mulch is put on top of the old. So there's no hauling compost from the pile or bin to the garden.

One disadvantage of the zero-tillage method is that the soil is later to warm up in the spring, so crops can get a later start. Since spring comes late to the Cape and Islands to begin with, this can mean that warm weather crops such as tomatoes, peppers and eggplant won't do well if planted before early June. Another disadvantage of the no-till method is that plants don't get the jumpstart that the loosened soil provides for roots. Finally, it's more difficult to rearrange the planting rows, or grow things like salad greens in blocks of plants.

Those who till the soil have the opportunity to loosen the earth, turn in soil amendments and rid the area of small weeds before planting. Tilled soil warms faster, an advantage given our cool springs, and the plants have an easy time growing roots quickly in the loose dirt. On the downside, the soil structure is destroyed with every tilling, it's hard work, and weed seeds get exposed to the light that triggers their germination.

Some decide to till every other year, or every third year, while others pick one method and stick with it.

These tomato supports were used for many years in the Cape Cod Cooperative Extension's demonstration gardens at the Barnstable County Fairgrounds. There the vegetables are planted in raised beds. Visiting this garden during the fair can be a great way to learn which vegetables grow well in this region.

THE FOLLOWING VEGETABLES DO WELL ON THE CAPE & ISLANDS

ASPARAGUS (*Asparagus officinalis*) Look for male asparagus plants such as Jersey Giant, Jersey King, or Jersey Knight. Males grow more edible shoots since they are not putting energy into seeds. Keep your asparagus bed well weeded, amended annually with compost, and mulched. You can start limited harvesting of spears in the third or fourth year after planting.

Beans (*Phaseolus vulgaris*) Both bush beans and climbing beans grow well in this region. Plant seeds directly in the ground in late May or early June. Harvest beans every three days to keep the plants flowering and producing.

Beets (*Beta*) Since beets appreciate well-drained soils they do well in our sandy loam gardens. Beets can be planted from mid-April on, even into August for fall harvests. The young seedlings must be thinned to at least six inches apart or the beets won't form. Dust new seedlings with diatomaceous earth to prevent flea beetle, earwig and slug damage. (This only needs to be done once or twice while the seedlings are small.)

Broccoli (*Brassica oleracea* var. *italica*) Plant broccoli at least eighteen inches apart. From early June on, spray every week or two with either Bt or spinosad, using a "spreader sticker" such as Turbo to make sure the product stays on the leaf. This spray prevents cabbage looper damage. Harvest the first head with a slanted cut. Do not expect home-grown broccoli heads to be as large as store bought. Most broccoli plants will grow side shoots after the main head is harvested and these should be picked as they appear. Harvesting these side shoots every three days will not only provide many tender, tiny heads of broccoli, but will keep the plant producing into the fall. If these small heads are left to go to flower, however, the plant will stop producing. Broccoli, cabbage and Brussels sprouts are heavy feeders, so apply an organic fertilizer early in the spring to the area where they will be planted.

Brussels Sprouts (*Brassica oleracea* var. *gemmifera*) These are a bit more tricky to grow in this region because the formation of the sprout heads on the stem is dependent on cool weather. Some of our summers are hot, but others cool, and fall weather can be too warm for sprouts to form. Gardeners who have limited space might want to avoid Brussels sprouts since the harvest can be more unreliable than many other vegetables.

Carrots (*Daucus carota* subsp. *sativus*) As long as your soil is loose and fairly free of rocks, carrots will grow well in this area. Those who have heavier clay or wet soils should grow carrots in raised beds that are filled with a sandy loam. Look for seeds of 'Nantes' types and plant in May spaced two or three inches apart. If seeds are sown more closely together they must be thinned so that the roots have room to grow. Carrots can also be sown in mid to late July for fall and winter harvests.

CHARD (*Beta vulgaris* subsp. *vulgaris*) Because chard can be harvested by cutting off the larger, outer leaves all summer it's one of the longest producing crops you can grow. Plant seeds six inches apart, either in the spring or in mid-summer for an autumn harvest. Chard can be used in any recipe that calls for spinach and it's far more productive.

CUCUMBER (*Cucumis sativus*) Cucumbers come in bush or vining varieties. Grow the vining types up a support to save space; it's a good plant to place under a pea trellis because once the peas stop producing the cucumbers can use the same space. The biggest problem for cucumbers is bacterial wilt that is spread by the yellow-and-black-striped cucumber beetle. Grow from seed or plants, looking for varieties like pickling or 'County Fair' that tend to be more disease-resistant. Cucumbers can also get powdery mildew – spray with an organic fungicide regularly through the season to control that fungal problem.

EGGPLANT (*Solanum melongena*) When I first moved to Cape Cod twenty-five years ago I was told that eggplant and peppers didn't grow well here because of the cooling sea breeze. Now, I grow both of these crops quite successfully in my garden although they are less successful if we have a cool or rainy summer. Look for 'Black Beauty' as a general, full-sized eggplant that is quite productive. Stake plants with heavy fruit.

GARLIC (*Allium sativum*) Garlic grows especially well for those who have sandy soil. Buy seed garlic in the fall and plant it between the end of September and late October. Break the head of garlic into individual cloves and place them in a shallow trench, spacing them about six inches apart. Cover with two to three inches of soil. The young garlic will sprout in three to six weeks. You can leave it uncovered all winter or protect it with a light application of saltmarsh hay or pine boughs. Do not cover with heavy mulch. When the curving flower buds start to appear, clip them off so that the plant puts all its energy into bulb production. Garlic gets harvested in early July, once the stems start to yellow. After garlic is harvested, plant other crops such as carrots, kale or chard in the newly open section of the garden.

GREEN BEANS (*Phaseolus vulgaris*) Grow green beans from seeds planted directly in the ground in late May. Beans should be picked every other day as they grow in order to keep the plants producing through the summer; if you only pick once a week or less often, the plants will stop flowering and producing more beans.

KALE (*Brassica oleracea* 'Lacinato') There are several varieties of kale but I've found that the most productive and delicious type for this area is Tuscan kale, also known as Lacinato or dinosaur kale. It can be grown from seed started indoors in late winter, or sown directly into the ground in early May or August. Thin to space plants eight inches apart, using the pulled young seedlings in your salads. Harvest only the largest outer leaves, letting the plants grow tall. In most winters we are still harvesting Tuscan kale to eat for our New Year's holiday meal. Spray as you do broccoli to control the cabbage looper larvae.

LEEKS (*Allium ampeloprasum* 'leek group') Leeks can be purchased as plugs, plants or seeds. Plugs or plants will produce harvestable leeks by late summer, while seed-grown leeks often mature into the fall and early winter. Place plants or seeds four to five inches apart.

LETTUCE (*Lactuca sativa*) Lettuce and arugula and mustards (*Brassicaceae* family) are best grown from seed, sowing every three or four weeks for continual harvest. You can scatter lettuce seeds over a small area and just pat in the soil or lightly cover the seed. When grown in this manner you can harvest young leaves daily, leaving some plants to grow larger and form heads if desired.

ONIONS (*Allium cepa*) There are three ways onions can be grown. You can start them indoors by seed in February, buy onion plants in May, or purchase small onion bulbs called "onion sets" in April. If you buy six packs of small onion plants be sure to carefully separate each small plant and space them six inches apart. If you plant them grouped, as they come in a pack from the garden center, they won't grow round onions but will only produce scallion-like growth.

PEAS (*Pisum sativum*) Do *not* plant your peas on Saint Patrick's Day; the soil is too cold on Cape Cod and the Islands for peas to germinate in March. Plant seeds from mid-April into mid-May and harvest from early June into July. Grow climbing varieties up fencing and harvest every two or three days for tender, flavorful peas. I've found that the sugar snap varieties are most productive and versatile.

PEPPERS (*Capsicum* varieties) For success with peppers on start seeds early indoors or buy plants. Pepper plants like heat so don't plant them outside too early. Look for varieties that mature in 80 to 90 days or less. In rainy summers pepper plants are prone to Septoria leaf spot, which mars the foliage but seldom kills the plants. Spray with one of the organic fungicides if you see spotted leaves and avoid frequent irrigation that splashes foliage.

POTATOES (*Solanum tuberosum*) If there was ever a great vegetable to grow in sandy soils, it's the potato. Plant them from pieces of seed potato in May. New baby potatoes can be harvested in late July and the main crop dug once the vines die down. The main pest of potato plants is the Colorado potato beetle; spray plants regularly with spinosad for control. Potatoes can be grown well in large fabric containers such as SmartPots.

SUMMER SQUASH (*Cucurbita* varieties) These plants take up a large amount of space, so plan accordingly. Spray regularly with an organic fungicide, coating stems and both sides of the leaf to delay and control powdery mildew. Male squash flowers open in the morning, followed by the females; plant flowers near the vegetable garden to attract pollinators to your squash. Harvest summer squash every other day when they are small for the best flavor and to stimulate more flowering.

TOMATOES (*Solanum lycopersicum*) Because tomatoes do best in hot, sunny weather and our summers can occasionally be cooler or rainy, we can have good tomato years in this region or bad ones. In general, planting several varieties will ensure a decent crop no matter what conditions Mother Nature delivers.

Although heirloom tomatoes are known for great taste, they tend to be more prone to leaf diseases and smaller crops. If you only have limited space you might want to grow an heirloom along with a couple hybrids.

The three most common problems people face when growing tomatoes here are blossom end rot, early blight, and tomato hornworms. Blossom end rot looks like a black scab on the bottom of the tomato fruit that's usually about the size of a quarter. Sometimes the black areas extend into the fruit itself. A common myth is that blossom end rot is caused by a lack of calcium, but the latest research shows that this isn't the cause. This condition is caused by stress to the plants, usually from shallow or uneven watering. BER is most frequently seen on the first tomatoes to ripen, but once the plants are larger and have deeper root systems, the scabs no longer mar the fruit. To prevent BER, water deeply less often, don't disturb the roots by tilling or hoeing next to the plants, and mulch the bed to keep soils cooler and evenly moist.

Early blight (*Alternaria solani*) is a fungus that kills tomato plants from the bottom up; the lower leaves start to show spots before turning yellow and dying. This condition moves up until the entire tomato plant is dead. Once early blight finds your garden there is no complete cure, but with the following procedures you'll be able to have a good crop of tomatoes despite the blight. First, take preventative measures to limit the fungus from getting onto the plants. 1) When planting young tomatoes, cut off any leaves that touch the ground. 2) Mulch around the young tomato seedlings immediately after planting so that rain or irrigation don't splash soil onto the foliage. 3) Start spraying every week to two weeks with an organic fungicide. There are several bacteria-based products on the market that work well. Note that there isn't a way to "treat the soil" so that all early-blight fungi get killed, and although grafted tomato plants are said to be more disease resistant, I have not found this to be the case when it comes to early blight.

Tomato hornworms are seldom a huge problem but occasionally gardeners will find several on their plants. Hornworms are large, fat and brilliant green with a spike on their backside. If your tomato foliage starts disappearing at a fast rate, as if animals are eating it, look for what appears to be black pepper on your plants. This is frass, aka hornworm poop. Hornworms may be hard to spot, but the best control is to pluck them off and either smash them, toss them into the woods, or put them on your birdfeeder for the crows and other birds to enjoy.

All vegetable gardeners have their favorites, but some of the more popular larger tomatoes in this region include: Better Boy, Celebrity, Early Girl, Oh Happy Day, and Virginia Sweets. Smaller varieties that do well are Mountain Magic (the most early-blight resistant tomato there is), Sungold (the sweetest cherry tomato) and the red cherry variety Sweet 100s.

When you buy tomato plants or seeds you might see a string of letters after the variety's name, and the words "determinate" or "indeterminate." The letters after a name indicate that it is a hybrid that has been bred to be resistant to various diseases that tomatoes are commonly prone to. The

Once garlic has been harvested in late June or early July, it can be hung in a shed or garage to dry. After about a week, cut the tops and roots off and store in a dark, cool place.

following is a list of the letters you may see on a package of tomato seeds, or on the label that comes with seedlings: V-Verticillium Wilt; F-Fusarium Wilt; FF-Fusarium, Races 1 & 2; N-Nematodes; T-Tobacco Mosaic Virus; A-Alternaria alternata; St-Stemphylium. Of these, it is most common to see varieties listed VF, which means that the plant is resistant to two of the most common fungi that attack tomatoes.

The terms "determinate" or "indeterminate" apply to how the tomato plants grow. Determinate plants will grow to a certain height and then stop. All the fruit on a determinate plant will be produced in a period that is about a month long. Tomatoes that are bred so that the bush stays small are determinate; examples are a variety called "patio and paste" or sauce tomatoes. Indeterminate types will continue growing and making new blossoms and fruit until the weather gets cold. These are the types of tomato plants that can grow over the tops of the cages and beyond stakes or other supports. Indeterminate varieties are good for those who want a constant supply of homegrown tomatoes for the table. Determinate types are good for people who want to can or freeze tomatoes so they can process lots of fruit at the same time.

Use a large, heavy-duty support for indeterminate tomatoes that's at least five feet tall. Small wire tomato cages are worthless and even the largest round supports will need the assistance of a stake to hold up healthy plants.

Once tomato plants stop producing fruit or wilt from frost, remove them from the garden and don't put any remains that were diseased in the compost.

WINTER SQUASH & PUMPKINS (*Cucurbita* varieties) Most varieties of winter squash and pumpkins take up a great deal of room and so are only appropriate for larger gardens. There are, however, some new varieties of butternut squash that are smaller. 'Honey Nut' and 'Honeybaby' are two that produce smaller fruit and vines, and are suitable to grow on trellises or other vertical supports. The main problem gardeners have with winter squash is powdery mildew. See the section above on summer squash for how to handle this fungal disease.

Chapter 9 *Perennial Vines*

WITH THE EXCEPTION OF most *Clematis*, perennial vines grow large, and so are best suited to planting on sizeable arbors rather than small trellises or garden gate archways. Even on big structures they need pruning for appearance and size management. Those who need a smaller vine or aren't prepared for ongoing maintenance should stick to *Clematis* or plant annual vines every year.

The arbor entry into Helen McVeigh's "bodacious cutting garden" is softened by clematis vines. Many Clematis *varieties can be shorter than most perennial vines, so they are suitable for smaller structures such as decorative arches and lampposts.*

CLEMATIS (*Clematis* hybrids and species) *Clematis* vines grow best in full sun. The old belief that they need their "feet in the shade" is a myth. They are fine in full sun although not particularly drought tolerant, so water these vines regularly. Some of these vines bloom on old wood, most notably *C. montana*, which flowers in the spring. Others bloom either exclusively on new growth or on both old and new. If you don't know which type you have, you can't go wrong by pruning them immediately after they bloom. Whether pruning your clematis right after flowering or cleaning up the tangle of growth in the spring, know that the new growth will come from the nodes below where you've pruned. So to promote more growth at the base of the plant, cut the old vines down low. If a plant has several stems, prune some low, others medium and a few at eye level to promote new growth from top to bottom. On the Cape and Islands *Clematis* can be slow to get established and are frequently prone to clematis wilt for a few years after planting. Clematis wilt is a fungal problem that occurs when the leaves or stems get damaged or wounded allowing various fungi to enter the plant. Typically, entire portions of the vine collapse, seemingly overnight. If this happens to your plant, remove the wilted stems and leaves. The plant can be sprayed with an organic fungicide but as *Clematis* become more established with mature root systems they are less likely to become infected and wilt.

SWEET AUTUMN CLEMATIS (*C. terniflora*) is one of the tallest vines although the flowers are small and in clusters. This plant has escaped into the wild, causing some to worry that it might be invasive. It is still sold in Massachusetts, however, and is somewhat shade-tolerant. The new variety called 'Sweet Summer Love' is smaller, has purple flowers, and requires full sun.

CLIMBING HYDRANGEA (*Hydrangea anomala* subsp. *petiolaris*) This vigorous vine climbs by both twining and aerial rootlets that stick onto structures, buildings or tree trunks. The flowers are white lacy clusters and the plant grows best in part to full shade. Flowers are formed the summer before it blooms, so do any pruning immediately after flowering or before the end of June. This vine can grow thirty to fifty feet high and it also makes an attractive groundcover.

HONEYSUCKLE (*Lonicera* species and hybrids) Although the Japanese honeysuckle (*Lonicera japonica*) is invasive and therefore banned for selling in Massachusetts, there are other varieties that are good landscape plants in the right situation. 'Goldflame' (*Lonicera* x *heckrottii*) is widely available and has bluish foliage with pink/yellow flowers.

WOODBINE HONEYSUCKLE (*Lonicera periclymenum*) varieties are highly fragrant and usually free of the powdery mildew that can disfigure the foliage on other species. Two popular, although often hard to find cultivars are

'Belgica' and 'Scentsation.' Both are highly fragrant and will repeat flower if deadheaded and pruned immediately after blooming.

TRUMPET HONEYSUCKLE (*Lonicera sempervirens*) is native to the south-eastern United States. Although the flowers aren't fragrant they are attractive to hummingbirds. Honeysuckle blooms in new growth so it can be pruned back as needed in early spring. Part shade to full sun.

TRUMPET VINE (*Campsis radicans*) This vine can be problematic because of its propensity to spread and its large size as the plant matures. In the right location and with the right care the flowers are stunning as well as a magnet for hummingbirds. Grow trumpet vine in full sun on strong structures and prune back hard in the early spring.

WISTERIA (*Wisteria* species and hybrids) Because it needs regular tending, this is a plant for gardeners, not home landscapers. All varieties of wisteria grow quite large and need big strong structures and a controlling

When a trumpet vine is in flower they are beautiful, but the vines grow large and often spread out from the roots, sprouting in random places nearby. Those who have a structure that is large enough to support them, and don't mind keeping them in check when they try and spread, are rewarded by their brilliant color blooms in mid-summer.

hand on the pruners. There are three types: Chinese (*W. sinensis*), Japanese (*W. floribunda*), and American (*W. frutescens*). The American is less rampant and more likely to reliably flower. Look for the varieties 'Amethyst Falls' (purple) or 'Nivea' (white). Newly-planted wisteria is famous for not flowering for years. Since a more stressful environment can sometimes stimulate flowering, prune the long green whips back hard every summer, keep the plant on the dry side, and don't fertilize.

Even when the climbing hydrangea is finished flowering it is a lovely vine. Be aware that this plant grows quite large, so be prepared to prune and train it as David Kirchner and Scott Warner have done here.

Chapter 10 *Hydrangeas*

HYDRANGEAS GET THEIR OWN chapter in this book for a few reasons. First of all, if there were a signature flower for the Cape and Islands it would probably be the blue mophead hydrangea. Plants with true-blue flowers are fairly rare, and the large blooms on hydrangeas make them especially impressive. Secondly, many types of hydrangeas flower for a long time, making them especially prized for summer landscapes. Finally, there

No matter which variety is used, the combination of weathered shingles and large hydrangea flowers is a classic look for summer on the Cape and Islands. Scott Warner and David Kirchner used Hydrangea arborescens *in the gardens surrounding their guest house.*

seem to be more questions and misconceptions about hydrangeas than any other shrub, so answers and information about this genus of plants are especially needed.

TYPES OF HYDRANGEAS Other than the climbing variety mentioned in the last chapter, there are several types of hydrangea that grow well in this region. Mopheads (*H. macrophylla*), lacecaps (*H. macrophylla* or *H. serrata*), smooth (*H. arborescens*), panicle (*H. paniculata*) and oakleaf (*H. quercifolia*). These different species vary primarily in the appearance of the flowers, how and when the blossoms are formed, and their preferences for moisture, sunlight or shade.

The blue (Penny Mac) and the purple (Glowing Embers) are examples of Hydrangea macrophylla, *the big leaf hydrangea. The white (Annabelle) is an* arborescens, *aka smooth hydrangea.*

This is one of the panicle hydrangeas, Hydrangea paniculata *'Pinky Winky.'*
Some panicles are cone-shaped and lacy, while others, such as 'Grandiflora' and
'Limelight,' are round and full.

WATER & SUN/SHADE The *macrophylla* and *serrata* groups tend to be
the thirstiest plants, followed by the *arborescens* species. You might notice
that your hydrangea wilts in the late afternoon on a hot day, only to perk up
again after sunset. When the temperatures are hot, water evaporates from
the leaves and flowers. This is called transpiration, and since the foliage and
flowers are large, the water often leaves the plant more quickly than the
plants can take it up through the roots. Water hydrangeas deeply every five
to seven days, and mulch around the plants to help hold moisture in the soil.

Panicle and oakleaf hydrangeas are more drought tolerant, but these
plants also benefit from a mulch layer. They also appreciate a deep soaking
once a week, but they are less likely to wilt on summer afternoons.

When it comes to plant placement, smooth hydrangeas and those in the
panicle group like part to full sun. If placed in too much shade these varieties won't flower well. Mophead and lacecap flowers last longest when the

plants are shielded from the strong mid-day sun. These need at least three hours of direct sun to flower well, but the blooms will keep their color longer when the plants are in morning or very late afternoon sun, but shaded through the noon hour.

FLOWER COLOR You can't change the color of the oakleaf, panicle or smooth hydrangeas. Oakleaf and panicle types start out white and turn various shades of pink as they age, according to their genetics. There are many new cultivars of *Hydrangea paniculata* that turn pale pink to bright rose-red in late summer and fall. 'Limelight,' a popular panicle type in this area, starts out a pale green, turns white and then becomes blushed with

Most mopheads and lacecaps can be altered from pink to blue, or from red to purple, but some are bred specifically to hold their pink color no matter what the pH of the soil happens to be. Check the label or research a hydrangea purchase online if you want a specific color for your garden.

pink in the fall. 'Vanilla Strawberry' and 'Pinky Winky' turn a darker pink on part of the flower head while other parts remain white, giving the plant an attractive, bi-color quality. 'Quick Fire' flowers earlier than most *paniculata* varieties, and the blooms turn dark pink.

Smooth hydrangeas that bloom white start off as pale green, mature to white and then go back to green as the blooms age. Pink blooming *arborescens* such as 'Invincibelle Spirit II,' 'Mini Mauvette' and 'Incrediball Blush' are various shades of pink through the summer. None of the oakleaf, panicle or smooth hydrangeas can be made blue.

Hydrangeas in the *macrophylla* and *seratta* groups, however, can often be changed from blue to pink or vice versa. Blue is developed when the soil is acidic and the plant is able to absorb aluminum. If the soil is alkaline, aluminum can't be absorbed and the flowers will be pink. For most people on the Cape and Islands the soil will be naturally acidic and they won't have to do anything to turn their mopheads or lacecaps blue.

If hydrangeas are growing near a lawn that's repeatedly limed, however, or if a particular town's water is highly alkaline and this has raised the pH of the soil over time, a blue hydrangea might turn pink or purple. The depth of color is genetically determined; a light blue will only turn light pink, never a deep blue or purple. White flowers will always be white.

Soil can be acidified by adding sulfur or aluminum sulfate. Use both according to the directions on the package, being careful not to over apply. Use lime to make soil alkaline. If lime is repeatedly applied on only one side, or on opposite quarters, of the shrub, and sulfur on the other side or quarters, the flowers will be a mix of blue and pink on the same plant.

Specifics for Mopheads & Lacecaps

Mopheads, aka big leaf hydrangeas, are the classic large, round, blue-or pink-flowered plants. Lacecaps are comprised of sterile and fertile flowers and look lacy, with a ring of sterile flowers with showy sepals resembling individual flowers around the tiny, fertile flowers on the inside. You may notice bees foraging on the inner flowers when the plants are in full bloom.

Mopheads and lacecaps grow from canes that come up from the roots, so they grow wider over time. Give all but the dwarf varieties a good six-foot diameter space when planting and expect them to grow taller. But

Hydrangea flowers last longest when cut in late August or September. Once the mopheads change from the fresh, sky-blue color to a softer grey-blue or shades of lavender, they will dry well. Panicle hydrangeas that are just turning pink will last well in fresh bouquets. Hydrangea flowers do not have to be hung upside down to dry them, but all leaves should be stripped off of the stems.

size aside, what's most important to understand about these hydrangeas is when their flowers are created. *H. macrophylla* and *H. serrata* form their flower buds in late summer for the following year. This is called "blooming on old wood."

Practically, this means that if the canes are cut back to "neaten the plants up" in the fall or spring, these hydrangeas will have few to no flowers the following summer. Since those buds, often invisible until the plant breaks dormancy, hold the germ of future flowers, they must survive the winter in order to bloom the following summer.

If the temperatures drop into the single digits or below zero during the winter these "old wood" buds get zapped and the plants will not bloom well the following summer. But it's not just cold that can kill the next season's flower. A very warm autumn can cause buds to swell prematurely and when a sudden drop in temperatures follows this, the germ of the flower can be destroyed. Similarly, a warm spell in February or March, followed by a plunge into the teens, can also kill the flower buds.

There are some varieties of *H. macrophylla* and *H. serrata* that flower heavily on old wood but also produce a few flowers on new growth. These are called remontant varieties and even after a cold winter or being cut to the ground they will bloom a bit in September or October. The most commonly available remontant hydrangeas at present are 'Endless Summer,' 'All Summer Beauty,' 'Penny Mac,' and 'Bloomstruck.' There are sure to be more introductions in the future as the plant breeders continue to select for this trait.

Mophead flowers last longest, and can be dried, when cut in late August or September. Any browned flowers can be removed by snipping just below the blossom. They can also be left on the plant over the winter and those that remain will be eliminated as you prune in May.

PROBLEMS SPECIFIC TO MOPHEAD OR LACECAP HYDRANGEAS

The most common problems on these plants include spotted leaves, distorted foliage, and flowers that turn brown quickly. These happen for three different reasons.

A hydrangea with this type of flower is called a lacecap.

Hydrangea macrophylla *varieties with round flowers are commonly called mopheads.*

When dark spots develop on the leaves in mid-summer, it is a leaf spot fungus. Frequent splashing of water on the foliage causes these spots. In a rainy summer it can't be avoided, but if an irrigation system is the cause, adjust it so the plants are watered longer but less often. Leaf spot is a cosmetic problem only and won't kill the plant.

Recently those growing hydrangeas have seen another situation that disfigures the leaves, but this one is an insect not a fungus. Chilli thrips (*Scirtothrips dorsalis*) have been identified by the UMass Plant Diagnostics Laboratory as being responsible for disfigured foliage on *Hydrangea macrophylla* plants on Cape Cod. Chilli thrips are very tiny insects that are pests on over 100 host plants, including many agricultural crops. So far the only chilli thrips damage in this area has been to hydrangeas.

Chilli thrips distort the leaves, making some look crinkled, with silver or dark webbing, and often red to brown edges. Other thrips and some mites can cause leaves to look similarly. If you see leaves that look distorted and are not a clear green in mid-summer, be sure to clean up all leaf litter around the plant in the fall and early spring. Chilli thrips overwinter in

Hydrangeas

This is how Chilli Thrips damage appears on hydrangea foliage.

such debris around the plant, and disposing of the leaves, weeds and other plant matter can help control this insect. Since this is such a new pest in the area, be sure to periodically check with the Cape Cod Cooperative Extension in Barnstable for updates on the spread and treatment of these insects.

The third problem, wilting and browning of hydrangea flowers, is usually due to the shrubs being grown in full or strong noonday sun. Petals will dry up if they wilt frequently in hot sunshine. To avoid early browning of hydrangea flowers, place the shrubs where they are shaded from eleven o'clock to four o'clock. Other possible causes of browning leaves or flowers include the application of too much aluminum sulfate, fertilizer, or herbicides.

Occasionally people will find cottony scale on the underside of their hydrangea leaves. Spray these with horticultural oil. Another infrequent pest is the small, green fruit worm that chews the leaves; control these with spinosad.

PRUNING MOPHEAD & LACECAP HYDRANGEAS

Let's start out with this hard truth: you can't make them shorter. A *macrophylla* or *serrata* hydrangea will replace its height in one season. So the plant that's growing over your windows one summer will do exactly the same thing the following summer whether you trim them down in the fall or spring. Not only will they be just as tall, or taller, by mid-July, but you'll have a dome of green growth on top that will cover the few flowers that bloom below. If a hydrangea is too tall for the location where it's planted, move it and plant a smaller cultivar in that place.

The best time to prune mopheads and lacecaps is in mid-May. If you prune hydrangeas in April you may be removing canes that would have blossomed had they been left in place. But by mid to late May the buds that survived the winter will have leaves opening and you can clearly see which canes are living and which ones are dead. Cut out any canes that have no green growth on them. If the top of the cane is bare, but there are leaves below, cut out the dead part but leave all green foliage.

In some years the canes will have died completely during the winter. When this happens the dead stems should get cut to within two or three inches of the ground, but watch for buds at the very base of the plant.

This is a classic example of a Nikko Blue hydrangea that was cut down in the spring or fall "to neaten it up" or to try and make it shorter. By July the shrub has grown just as high as the previous year, and it has very few flowers.

Hydrangeas

When you can see leaves starting to form on hydrangea canes in late May, it's time to prune. Once the leaves start growing, canes with buds that are still black or not opening up can be removed. Any cane that has leaves forming on it should be left because that's where your flowers will form for the coming summer.

These are often so protected that they will grow and flower after the most extreme winters.

HOW TO PRUNE MOPHEAD & LACECAP HYDRANGEAS

☙ Prune these plants in late May when you can clearly see what's living and what's dead. Wait to prune or clean them up until the buds have opened into leaves that are about the size of a quarter.

☙ Clip off any remaining flowers from the previous year.

☙ Begin by removing any bare canes that have no green growth on them. Do not be fooled by buds that have a touch of green on them, or the green that shows if you scratch the stems. When other stems have leaves that are opening, remove all canes that don't contain such growth.

☙ Some stems will be bare on top but have leaves opening on the bottom of the canes; prune off the top bare sections by cutting about an inch above the first set of leaves you come to.

☙ Remove any weak canes that are curved and lying on the ground.

☙ Now stop: do not try and make them shorter; if your hydrangeas are too tall for the location where they are growing, your next step is to dig them up and relocate the plants to a better location.

The most common problem for smooth hydrangeas such as 'Annabelle' is the hydrangea leaftier. Look for top leaves that look like small packets that never open up. Clip these off and destroy them to kill the larvae that are inside.

One of the most popular smooth hydrangeas is 'Annabelle.' The flowers are so large on this shrub that they will bend over, especially after a rainfall. No pruning or fertilizing will correct this. If you don't want your flowers to bend over, put a stake in the center of the plant and run twine around individual stems, pulling them up to the position that they look best, and returning the string back around the center stake before taking it out and around another stalk.

This method of staking will keep the plant's natural appearance while holding individual stems at different angles. It is more attractive and functional than wrapping a cord around the outside of the entire plant.

SPECIFICS FOR SMOOTH HYDRANGEAS Smooth hydrangeas flower on new growth so they aren't affected by cold winters. They will also bloom after a hard pruning, but the lower *H. arborescens* are cut, the more likely the flowers are to flop toward the ground on new stems. This is particularly true for the large flowering types like 'Annabelle' and 'Incrediball,' which often have to be supported with staking.

These hydrangeas typically spread out to all sides and grow four to five feet tall. They can be divided and the spreading growth removed or transplanted, but in general their height will be in the five foot range, and their width will continue to double, so be sure to site them accordingly.

Prune smooth hydrangeas anytime in the spring, first removing deadwood, next taking away two or three of the oldest canes close to the ground, and then cleaning up the plant by clipping them back by a foot or so. Like the mopheads and lacecaps, you cannot keep a mature plant shorter because they will replace their height in one summer.

Hydrangeas in the paniculata, *or panicle group form their flowers on the ends of new growth, so they can be pruned back in the late fall or early spring. Prune these plants before the stems form leaves in May. Don't do much pruning after mid-May as that can reduce the number of blooms. The* H. paniculata *pictured is Bobo, one of the shorter cultivars that are good for foundation plantings or containers.*

Grow smooth hydrangeas in part shade to full sun. The pink-flowering varieties such as 'Invincibelle Spirit II' appreciate more sun. Some plants will produce new flowers if the faded ones are promptly cut away from the plant.

In May and June on the lookout for the hydrangea leaftier on these plants. You'll notice that the top leaves are knitted into bundles or tied together on their edges. If you pry the foliage apart you'll see a greenish brown larvae,

Olethreutes ferriferana, inside. Since they are protected inside the leaves it's difficult to spray so that they'll be eliminated. The best control is to cut these off and destroy them by smashing or throwing them in the garbage.

SPECIFICS FOR THE PANICLE GROUP Hydrangeas in the *paniculata* group like more sun than the other species. These are the most drought-tolerant hydrangeas, but the flowers last longest and the plants grow strongest when they are well watered once a week.

Plant these in full or part sun and choose a plant for each location based on its mature size. Varieties such as 'Grandiflora,' 'Tardiva,' 'Vanilla Strawberry' and 'Limelight' grow quite large and can even be pruned to be multi-stemmed small trees. 'Pinky Winky' is also a big plant but a bit more up-

The native oakleaf hydrangeas are valued for their brilliant fall color as well as their flowers and attractive bark.

right than the others. 'Little Lime' and 'Zinfin Doll' top out at about five feet tall, and 'Little Quickfire,' 'Bobo,' or 'Bombshell' stay the smallest at around three feet high.

Prune these hydrangeas in the spring in the following manner: first remove any dead branches. Next, look for branches that are headed into the center of the plant instead of out, away from the middle; follow those stems back to where they join another and cut them leaving a half-inch stub. After that, look for crossed branches that are rubbing and remove one of those, again following the stem you're cutting back to where it joins another. Finally, trim back for shape, from the top down, cutting the outer stems lower and the center ones higher to create a rounded plant.

Mal and Mary Kay Condon used to own The Hydrangea Nursery on Nantucket. Recently they have created another hydrangea heaven on Cape Cod that showcases many varieties of these beautiful shrubs.

'Knockout' roses flower along the fence in gardens designed by artists Willow Shire and Jaime daLomba. Plant all Knockout roses where they can grow five feet tall and six feet wide.

Browned flowers can be cut off in the fall or left through the winter according to your preference.

SPECIFICS FOR OAKLEAF HYDRANGEAS The oakleaf hydrangea (*Hydrangea quercifolia*) thrives in moist soil in full sun to part shade. When grown in part sun, the fall foliage is red to burgundy, and the exfoliating bark is attractive in the winter. This plant suckers to the sides, growing five to six feet tall and sometimes twice as wide. Like those in the *macrophylla* group, the flowers are formed the summer before it blooms. This is a plant that is a little looser in form than other hydrangeas, and is a good component of a mixed flowering shrub border. 'Snow Queen' is a variety that's a bit shorter but has large flowers that age pink. There are also cultivars that stay shorter, such as 'Pee Wee' and 'Ruby Slippers.'

Chapter 11 *Roses*

Next to hydrangeas, people on the Cape and Islands love their roses. Most come into flower in late June, and some either continue to flower or repeat bloom in early fall. Roses need to be planted where they will receive at least six hours of dead-on sun including the noon hour. Other keys to success with roses include amending the soil in a wide area with compost or aged manure, fertilizing two or three times in a summer with an organic rose food, and a deep soaking once a week.

Roses get pruned in the spring when the forsythia blooms. The first step for all types is to cut out dead wood. Hybrid teas and climbing roses are

Irwin and Cindy Ehrenreich grow dozens of roses of all types in their gardens in Barnstable.

Those who want disease-resistant, repeat-flowering roses that stay shorter should look for plants in the 'Flower Carpet' or 'Drift' series.

then pruned back to just above an outward facing bud so that the new growth on the top of the canes will move away from the center of the plant. Remember that roses flower at the end of the new growth, and each of the red buds on the canes in spring will grow into a stem with flowers on the end. So the shorter you prune a rose and the more of those red buds you take off, the fewer flowers you'll have that summer.

Prune established climbing roses by cutting one or two of the oldest, thickest canes down around six inches high. Next cut some of the stems to two to four feet high, and others just trimmed a little off the top. Using this "shotgun" approach will stimulate new growth in all areas, so you're more likely to have flowers from the near the bottom of the plant up to the top. If you never cut any of the canes short, the plant ends up with all the flowers at the top of your trellis or arbor and nothing at eyelevel or below.

There are many varieties of shrub or landscape roses that repeat flower and are less prone to diseases such as mildew and black spot. Short to medium varieties include 'The Fairy,' 'Drift,' 'Oso Easy,' and 'Flower Carpet' series, while most of the 'Meidiland' and 'Knockout' roses grow taller and wider. There are others too numerous to mention, and new cultivars are released every year. These plants don't have to be deadheaded, but often their looks are improved and repeat flowering stimulated if the old flowers are promptly removed.

Other types of roses such as the hybrid teas and floribundas should be deadheaded although not all will produce more flowers. It isn't necessary to "cut down above a set of five leaflets" as the old deadheading myth says. Clipping spent blossoms just below the wilted flower is faster and gets rid of any developing seeds.

ROSE PROBLEMS The biggest problems for roses in this area are black spot and larvae. Black spot is a fungal disease that is most pronounced when we've had a cool, wet spring. Since cool and damp pretty much describes our typical spring weather in this region, roses that are especially susceptible to black spot will usually have this disease.

Most landscape shrub roses are fairly resistant to black spot and in most years the damage to these plants will be minor. But after an extremely wet and cool spring even these plants can show the yellowing and spotted leaves typical of the disease. Like most fungal diseases, it's best to spray vulnerable plants before they show signs of a problem. Use a fungicide labeled for black spot according to directions. There are several organic, bacterial-based fungicides such as Actinovate, Serenade, and Revitalize that can be used for those who take a "least toxic" approach in their gardens.

There are also organic treatments for larvae damage. The two main pests

'Collette' is a variety of climbing rose that is fragrant, repeat flowering and disease resistant.

of roses are the winter moth and rose slug larvae. Winter moth caterpillars hatch out between late March and the end of April, and they feed into June. The main damage is done as they grow larger and take bigger bites of the rose foliage. Spraying with spinosad after the foliage is open is the best treatment, and one or two applications are usually all that is needed.

The rose slug is not a slug but a small green caterpillar similar to the winter moth larvae, except instead of chomping right through a leaf they

Coral flowers fill the 'Climbing America' rose in late June. This variety is especially suitable for smaller trellises, arbors and fences.

scrape the bottom tissues away from the veins. If your rose foliage suddenly is turning white and looking skeletonized in June, you have this bud worm. Again, spinosad is the treatment of choice, making sure to spray it under the leaves to coat the bottom of the foliage as well as possible.

Occasionally people have trouble with Japanese beetles on roses. These are easy to knock by hand into a plastic carton filled with an inch of cooking oil. To control future populations, apply milky spore (*Paenibacillus popilliae*), a bacterium, to your lawn as the package directs and don't water your turf too frequently. Beetles like to lay their eggs in damp soil, so irrigating every other day is like inviting grubs and beetles onto your property.

ROSES & WINTER Clean up fallen leaves and other debris around roses in the fall to help control black spot and mildew. Plants that were badly infected in a given year should be sprayed with a fungicide in November or early December to help suppress the fungi.

Those who grow hybrid tea roses often protect the graft at the base of the plants with composted manure in the fall. Pile the manure up about eight inches against the stems in November. Pull this away from the stem in early April, spreading it over the surface of the soil under the rosebush to amend the soil for the summer. Although shrub roses would benefit from the soil improvement that compost or manure offers, they do not need graft protection.

If a rose has extremely long canes that might whip around in winter winds, these can be cut back by a third to a half in the fall. Most roses, however, do not get pruned in the fall; for all but the tallest plants, wait until spring for rose pruning.

In late June and early July many buildings on the Cape and Islands are filled with flowering roses. Nantucket is particularly known for the roof-top trellises and rose-filled landscapes in the summer.

Chapter 12 *Shrubs*

THERE ARE SO MANY SHRUBS that do well in this region that instead of listing a selection of plants I'm grouping them according to their average use in the landscape. Feel free to mix and match, of course. You might, for example, place a larger shrub that's listed in the chapter on screening off the corner of a house, or in front of a windowless wall in a foundation planting.

When planting any shrub, research the average size of a ten-year-old plant and then space accordingly. Most people place plants too close together so that it instantly looks full, but in three to four years the plants are too crowded. Shrubs that are spaced correctly require the least maintenance; you won't have to prune them to try to slow their growth.

Ninebark (Physocarpus) *varieties are available in a variety of sizes and foliage colors. This variety, 'Centerglow,' is one of the larger growing types that have burgundy leaves.*

Weigelas are available in assorted sizes and foliage colors. Some weigelas bloom in June and others repeat flower later in the summer.

I have not included shrubs in this list that have proven to be short-lived, prone to insects and diseases, or are marginally hardy. I have included many plants with foliage that is not green. When planting shrubs, aim for a selection of different colors and textures of leaves so that even if nothing is in flower, you'll still have a colorful garden.

Fothergilla shrubs flower in late April and have brilliant fall foliage as well. The varieties called 'Blue Mist' and 'Blue Mist Dwarf' also have frosty blue leaves in the summer.

FOUNDATION PLANTINGS & SMALLER SHRUBS FOR FLOWER BORDERS

The way that most people get into trouble with foundation plantings is by choosing shrubs that are instantly the ideal size so they look like the perfect height and width when they are put in place. The problem is, of course, that these plants grow larger. Soon what looked perfect on planting is covering the windows or needs to be sheared into green meatball shapes to try and slow down the growth. If you want less work, choose plants that might look small initially and space them for their future growth. Plant perennials or annuals in between such shrubs to make the beds look fuller while the shrubs grow. Also, place foundation plants three to four feet out from the house, depending on their projected size.

SMALLER DECIDUOUS SHRUBS

Blue mist fothergilla (*Fothergilla gardenii* 'Blue Mist' and 'Blue Mist Dwarf') Sun to part shade.

Butterfly bush (*Buddleia davidii*) Sun.

'Chardonnay Pearls' deutzia (*Deutzia gracilis* 'Chardonnay Pearls') Sun to part shade.

Diervilla (*Diervilla rivularis* and x *splendens* 'Kodiak,' 'Firefly,' 'Nightglow' and others) Sun to shade.

Dwarf deutzia (*Deutzia crenata* 'Nikko') Sun to part shade.

Dwarf hydrangeas (*Hydrangea* in variety) Especially noteworthy are 'Bobo,' 'Little Quickfire,' 'Let's Dance Diva,' 'CityLine Rio,' and 'Let's Dance Rave.' Part sun to part shade.

Dwarf viburnums Varieties including Korean spice (*V. carlesii*), densa (*V. obovatum* 'Densa'), 'Wabi-Sabi' (*V. plicatum tomentosum* 'Wabi-Sabi') and 'Lil' Ditty' Witherod Viburnum (*V. cassinoides* 'Lil' Ditty'). Sun to part sun.

Golden privet (*Ligustrum* 'Sunshine') Sun to part sun.

Dwarf summersweet (*Clethra alnifolia* 'Hummingbird' or 'Sixteen Candles') Sun to part shade.

Dwarf lilacs (*Syringa* varieties 'Lilac,' 'Scent and Sensibility,' 'Miss Kim' and 'Bloomerang') Sun.

Japanese spirea (*Spirea japonica* varieties including 'Magic Carpet,' the 'Double Play' series, and 'Golden Elf.' Sun to part sun.

'Little Henry' sweetspire (*Itea virginica* 'Little Henry') Sun to shade.

Miniature mock orange (*Philadelphus x virginalis* 'Dwarf Snowflake') Sun.

Ninebark (*Physocarpus opulifolius* varieties 'Lady in Red,' 'Tiny Wine,' 'Lil' Devil') Sun to part sun.

Weigela (*Weigela florida* varieties such as 'Sonic Bloom,' 'Summer Wine,' and 'Java Red') Sun.

Yellow spirea (*Spirea thunbergii* 'Ogon') Fine yellow foliage, white flowers. Sun.

SMALLER EVERGREEN SHRUBS Although most dwarf evergreens grow quite slowly, some grow in width fairly quickly. Be sure to check the mature size and then add a foot or two onto that when you're considering what to plant. Many dwarf evergreens don't look good if repeatedly sheared. A good example is the golden cypress that has thread-like foliage; 'Gold Thread' and 'Gold Mop' grow five to six feet tall and are usually wider than they are tall. When they are placed in the wrong location people often resort to shearing them in an attempt to keep the plant smaller, but this removes the very feature that made the shrub attractive in the first place.

Dwarf Alberta spruce (*Picea glauca* 'Conica') Sun to part shade.

Dwarf balsam fir (*Abies balsamea* 'Nana') Sun to part shade.

Dwarf Hinoki false cypress (*Chamaecyparis obtusa* 'Compacta' or 'Nana') Sun to part shade.

Dwarf holly (*Ilex* varieties such as 'Little Rascal,' 'Scallywag,' and 'Castle Wall') Sun to part shade.

Dwarf Norway spruce (*Picea abies* 'Pumila') Sun to part sun.

Dwarf rhododendron (*Rhododendron yakushimanum* and others. 'Ken Janeck,' 'Yaku Prince,' 'Yaku Princess,' 'Yaku Angel,' and 'Percy Wiseman' are common.) Part sun to shade.

Dwarf white pine (*Pinus strobus* varieties including 'Minuta,' 'Soft Touch,' and 'Blue Jay') Sun to part shade.

Globe blue spruce (*Picea pungens* 'Globosa') Sun to part sun.

Globe Japanese cedar (*Cryptomeria japonica* 'Globosa Nana') Sun to part sun.

Gold thread or mop cypress (*Chamaecyparis pisifera* varieties) Sun to part sun.

Inkberry holly (*Ilex glabra*) Sun to part sun.

Japanese holly (*Ilex crenata* 'Soft Touch,' 'Hellerii,' 'Compacta,' and others) Sun to part shade.

'Otto Luyken' cherry laurel (*Prunus laurocerasus* 'Otto Luyken' and other varieties) Sun to part shade.

Skimmia (*Skimmia japonica*) Shade to part shade.

Upright Japanese plum yew (*Cephalotaxus harringtonia* 'Fastigiata') Part sun or part shade.

Variegated boxwood (*Buxus sempervirens* 'Variegata') Sun to part shade.

SHRUBS FOR EXPOSED LOCATIONS The following shrubs and trees tolerate the windy conditions on ocean or lake front properties. Plant these in locations where wind and salt spray are common. Most of these plants are available in several cultivars so check to see which variety is best suited for the place where you're planting. All of these grow well in sun or part sun, and the yew, summersweet and hinoki false cypress will also grow in part shade. Note that these are also good plants for along roadways that are salted in the winter.

Arrowwood viburnum (*Viburnum dentatum*) Sun to part shade.

Bayberry (*Myrica pensylvanica*) Sun to part shade.

Beach plum (*Prunus maritima*) Sun to part sun.

Bearberry (*Archtostaphylos uva-ursi*) Sun to part sun.

Euonymus (*Euonymus japonicus*) Sun to part sun.

Hinoki false cypress (*Chamaecyparis obtusa*) Sun to part shade.

Japanese black pine (*Pinus thunbergii*) Sun.

Japanese spirea (*Spirea japonica*) Sun to part shade.

Junipers (*Juniperus* most species and cultivars, including Red Cedar *J. virginiana*) Sun to part sun.

Mugo pine (*Pinus mugo*) Sun to part sun.

Pink Spirea (*Spirea japonica*) Sun to part sun.

Privet (*Ligustrum* most species) Sun to part shade.

Rose of Sharon (*Hibiscus syriacus*) Sun.

Salt bush, aka groundsel (*Baccharis halimifolia*) Sun.

Summersweet (*Clethra alnifolia*) Sun to part shade.

Yew (*Taxus cuspidata*) Sun to part shade.

Groundsel (Baccharis halimifolia) *comes into flower in late September and thrives in exposed locations where other shrubs might die.*

Chapter 13
Shrubs & Trees for Screening

SINCE MOST PEOPLE WANT to have some degree of privacy for their landscapes, many homeowners look for plants that will quickly screen them from the neighbors or passersby. This has led to a plague of the Leyland cypress on the Cape and Islands, a tree that is problematic in terms of winter damage, maintenance, ultimate size, and disease. For these reasons you will not see this tree on my list of recommended plants for screening. If you need huge, fast growth, the 'Green Giant' arborvitae (*Thuja* 'Green Giant') is a far better choice.

These two plants aside, however, I'd encourage anyone needing screening not to plant a row of one type of shrub or tree. Every year new insects and diseases make their way into our region, and should one of these migrant pests happen to target the plant you've chosen for your screening, you could lose your entire barrier.

Additionally, most properties don't need the same height of screening all the way around the yard, and a wall of tall evergreens can make a property feel smaller and claustrophobic. Taller plants may be needed only in selected spaces to provide privacy for a deck or patio, for example, while a group of shorter shrubs might work in the back or around corners.

There are areas that might need evergreen plants that need evergreen screening, while other spaces only require protection in the summer. If a privacy planting is composed of a variety of colors and textures of plants, some evergreen and others deciduous, there will be something interesting going on with foliage and flowers all year.

When planning a mixed border for screening, stick to odd numbers. Use some groups of three, some singles, and a group of five if space allows. Plant the groupings in a staggered formation, threes in a triangle, for example, not lined up in a row. Arrange the plants so that different colors of foliage are next to each other, and the evergreens and deciduous alternate. For example, a dark green conifer might be followed by a deciduous shrub with

Taller deciduous shrubs such as Weigela *'Rubidor' and* Viburnum *'Summer Snowflake' make good screening plants that create privacy.*

light-green or variegated leaves, this next to a group of three broadleaf evergreens such as a holly, and those followed by a shrub with small, light -green leaves or needles. In such an arrangement if any one plant dies, you can put another plant in its place and your screening will still be attractive.

Evaluate the area screening plants will be planted in over the course of one day to get an accurate idea of how much sun the area receives. In general the plants listed here easily grow six feet and taller.

DECIDUOUS SHRUBS FOR SCREENING

Bottlebrush buckeye (*Aesculus parviflora*) Shade to part shade.

Doublefile viburnum (*Viburnum plicatum tomentosum* 'Mariesii' or 'Summer Snowflake') Sun to part shade.

Dream Catcher beauty bush (*Kolkwitzia amabilis* 'Maradco') Sun to part sun.

'Exbury' azalea (*Rhododendron* sp. 'Knaphill' and 'Exbury') Sun to part shade.

Forsythia (*Forsythia* x *intermedia* hybrids) Sun to part shade.

Golden privet (*Ligustrum* x *vicaryi*) Sun to part sun.

Hydrangeas (*Hydrangea* species and varieties such as 'Tardiva' and 'Quick Fire' are especially fast growing. 'Lime Light,' 'Pinky Winky,' 'Vanilla Strawberry,' and 'Nikko Blue') Sun to part shade.

Ninebark (*Physocarpus opulifolius* 'Diablo' and 'Centerglow') Sun to part sun.

Purple smoke bush (*Cotinus coggygria* 'Royal Purple' or 'Grace') Sun to part sun.

River birch (*Betula nigra* 'Heritage') Sun to part shade.

Rose of Sharon (*Hibiscus syriacus*) Sun to part sun.

Weigela (*Weigela florida* taller varieties) Sun to part sun.

Witchhazel (*Hamamelis* varieties including x *intermedia* 'Arnold Promise') Sun to part sun.

By using a variety of flowering shrubs in a mixed screen you can have flowers in almost every month of the year. This 'Arnold Promise' witchhazel blooms in late February and March.

When Leyland Cypresses are sheared regularly they can be maintained as an attractive hedge. These trees do, however, keep growing. Helen McVeigh has named this group her "Great Wall of Leyland."

EVERGREEN PLANTS FOR SCREENING

Andromeda (*Pieris japonica*) Shade to part shade.

Arborvitae (*Thuja* – 'Emerald Green' for small spaces, 'Green Giant' for large) Sun to part sun.

Cryptomeria (*Cryptomeria japonica* 'Yoshino') Sun to part sun.

Hinoki false cypress (*Chamaecyparis obtusa* 'Gracilis' or 'Crippsii') Sun to part shade.

Holly including Nellie Stevens (*Ilex* 'Nellie Stevens'), Blue Maid (*Ilex* x *meserveae* 'Blue Maid'), and American (*Ilex opaca*). Sun to part shade.

Junipers including eastern red cedar (*Juniperus virginiana*) and Chinese junipers such as 'Hetzii,' 'Robusta' (*Juniperus chinensis*) Sun.

PJM rhododendron (*Rhododendron* x 'PJM') Sun to part shade.

Rhododendrons (*Rhododendron* varieties) Part sun to shade.

Skip laurel (*Prunus laurocerasus* 'Schipkaensis') Part shade. Not for windy, exposed locations or in direct sun in the winter.

Upright yew (*Taxus* x *media* 'Hicksii' or *T. cuspidata* 'Capitata') Sun to part shade.

Weeping Alaskan cedar (*Chamaecyparis nootkatensis* 'Pendula') Sun to part shade.

Cryptomeria, holly, spruce, arborvitae and assorted deciduous trees form a lovely mixed screening border for this Island property.

Chapter 14 *Trees*

Because dappled willows are grafted onto their trunks, they stay smaller than most trees. Buy one that has a trunk at the correct height because although the branches will grow taller and wider, the trunk itself doesn't get higher.

ALTHOUGH FLOWERING TREES and smaller specimens get the most attention from homeowners, don't ignore the beauty of our native oaks, wild cherry (*Prunus virginiana*), sassafras (*Sassafras albidum*), and pines. These plants support many species of wildlife and give our landscapes their singular, seaside look.

No matter what variety of tree that is being grown, here are some basic tips for planting and care.

- Be sure not to plant trees too deeply. Make sure the root flare, where the trunk spreads out at a slight angle before meeting the ground, is visible. If the trunk goes straight into the soil, it's probably too deep.
- In general, go easy on the fertilizer. A light application of organic fertilizer once a year under the drip line is sufficient. A light application of compost, mulch or chopped leaves is even better.
- Do not pile mulch against the trunk of a tree. Feather the mulch out a few inches away from the trunk and root flare.

Kousa dogwoods grow well on the Cape and Islands. Many have creamy white flowers but a few have red or pink blossoms. This is 'Satomi,' a common pink variety.

- Prune trees by removing deadwood and crossed branches. Make light cuts to improve appearance but avoid shearing and topping trees.
- If newly planted trees are staked, remove those supports after the first six to eight months. Trees grow stronger root systems when they are allowed to sway in the wind.
- Water a tree deeply, once a week, using a sprinkler or soaker hoses in times of drought. Water the entire area under the drip line, not just the base of the trunk.
- The light green "moss" you see on branches doesn't hurt trees. This is lichen, which is a composite organism of multiple fungi and algae. It is living on the trees but takes nothing from them. Lichen often flourishes on trees that have reduced canopies because of other stresses, however. Attempting to remove the lichen can cause harm to the tree.

The seven-son flower on the left and the redbud on the right are two attractive small trees that should be planted more frequently. Even when they are not in flower they are appealing in the garden.

LOW-MAINTENANCE TREES FOR CAPE LANDSCAPES

American holly (*Ilex opaca*) Native evergreen. Sun to part shade.

Blue atlas cedar (*Cedrus atlantica* 'Glauca') Evergreen with blue color needles. Sun.

Carolina silverbell (*Halesia carolina*) Sun to part sun.

Concolor fir (*Abies concolor*) Evergreen, better than blue spruce in this region. Sun.

Cornelian cherry (*Cornus mas* and *C. officinalis*) Sun to part sun.

Crabapple (*Malus*, disease-resistant cultivars) Sun.

Dappled willow (*Salix integra* 'Hakuro Nishiki') Variegated, grafted small tree. Sun to part sun.

Fringetree (*Chionanthus virginicus*) Sun to part shade.

Ginkgo (*Ginkgo biloba*) Sun to part sun.

Golden rain tree (*Koelreuteria paniculata*) Sun to part sun.

Green giant arborvitae (*Thuja standishii* x *plicata* 'Green Giant') Large, fast-growing evergreen. Sun to part shade.

Japanese red maple (*Acer palmatum* 'Bloodgood' and others) Part sun to shade.

Japanese snowbell (*Styrax japonicus*) Sun to part shade.

Japanese stewartia (*Stewartia pseudocamellia*) Sun to part shade.

Japanese tree lilac (*Syringa reticulata*) Early summer flowering. Sun to part sun.

Kanzan cherry (*Prunus* 'Kanzan') Spring flowers in bubblegum pink. Sun to part sun.

Katsura (*Cercidiphyllum japonicum*) Sun to part sun.

Kousa dogwood (*Cornus kousa*) Early summer flowering. Sun to part shade.

Oaks, red and white (*Quercus rubra, Quercus alba*) Native. Sun to part sun.

Paperbark maple (*Acer griseum*) Ornamental bark. Sun to part shade.

Red maple (*Acer rubrum*) Native with red flowers in spring. Sun to part shade.

Redbud (*Cercis canadensis*) Native. Colored-leaf cultivars available. Part sun to part shade.

River birch (*Betula nigra* 'Heritage') Fast-growing native with ornamental bark. Sun to part sun.

Seven-son flower (*Heptacodium miconioides*) Fall flowering with ornamental bark. Sun to part shade.

Sourwood (*Oxydendrum arboreum*) Native with great fall color. Sun to part sun.

Sweetbay magnolia (*Magnolia virginiana*) Native and semi-evergreen. Sun to part shade.

Tulip tree (*Liriodendron tulipifera*) Native, large shade tree. Sun.

ABOVE: *Kanzan cherry trees are covered with large, bubblegum pink flowers in May. You will also see this tree listed as a Kwanzan cherry.*
BELOW: *Although they do have lacy yellow flowers, the seedpods are a showy feature on a golden rain tree.*

Chapter 15 *Lawns*

THERE ARE AS MANY TYPES of lawns as there are styles of gardens. Although the twentieth-century fashion was to have a property carpeted in a large monoculture of grass, this type of yard isn't for everyone. Lawns can be pure grass, mixed with white clover, or a combination of grasses and wild plants. It's up to homeowners to decide how much work, resources and products should go into their lawns, working within local and state laws and guidelines.

Keeping turf weed-free requires a range of herbicides that can be problematic or detrimental to our waterways and physical health. Several lawn chemicals that were commonly used in the past fifty years are now banned, and it's likely that as time goes on communities will outlaw more of such products. Lawn insecticides and fungicides can also be harmful, especially when used to excess.

Water usage will be an important issue in years to come, and it's likely that restrictions will be placed on lawn irrigation. Many believe that the costs, both monetarily and environmentally, of a monoculture of grass will be too expensive as we go into the future. So although I give the general advice about maintaining healthy turf, I believe that grass-only lawns of the late twentieth century will soon be a thing of the past.

Those open to a multi-plant lawn should consider seeding white clover in with the grass. Clover is a strong, dark-green plant that also has the ability to take nitrogen from the air and bring it into the soil. So a lawn in sandy soil will usually be greener if clover is mixed in with the grass.

SOD VS. SEED When installing a new lawn, you'll have a choice of sod or seed. Sod provides an instant lawn, but since most sod is made of bluegrass, this might influence your decision. Bluegrass is best in full sun, and needs a bit more in the way of water and fertilizer than other grasses.

The best seed for the Cape is a mix that is primarily fescues, with some perennial rye and a bit of bluegrass added. This mixture is good in full sun or part shade, withstands foot traffic, and greens up early in the spring. For lawns in part to full shade, a mix of fescues that is designed for lower-light areas is best. Those trying to keep grass growing in full shade might need to loosen bare areas and seed every April in order to keep these areas green.

The best time to seed a lawn is late August into late September. The second best time is from mid-April to late May. Sod can be laid anytime it's available, but in very hot summer weather or during rainy spells it might be harder to find. Newly sodded or seeded lawns need to be watered daily, but after a couple of weeds they should be weaned off of so much moisture. Transition them gradually to a longer soaking every four days. Established lawns do just fine with a long, deep watering every five to seven days.

FERTILIZING LAWNS I am partial to using organic fertilizers on lawns, applied in April and early September. If you're using a synthetic fertilizer at the right time, turf grasses use this very efficiently, however, so little runs off. Put synthetic fertilizer down in mid-May and early September. Do not use lawn products beyond October, even if they have "winter" in their name. Lawns are actively growing during the warm months of September and October, so early fall fertilization builds plant strength before the winter.

Lawns also benefit from an application of compost every year or two. This is especially important for lawns that are older, sparse, or growing in

If lawns are irrigated too frequently they are prone to a number of problems, including a variety of fungal conditions that can kill turf.

sandy soils. Apply between a half-inch to an inch right on the surface in the spring or fall. This can renew turf that's become thin because of poor soils, especially if the compost is applied after the area is aerated.

LIMING LAWNS Turf grasses thrive in neutral to slightly acidic soils, so it's good to keep your soil pH between 6.5 and 7.5. Although the Cape and Islands have naturally acidic soils, never assume that your lawn needs to be limed every year. Have a soil pH test done by the Cape Cod Cooperative Extension in Barnstable or at the UMass Soil Testing Lab every two to three years to determine if you need to lime or not. Lime can be applied anytime.

THE IRRITATION OF THE IRRIGATION Unfortunately, most automatic sprinkler systems are set up to go off too frequently to water too shallowly. Frequent watering is a prescription for moss, grubs, and every lawn disease in the book. Moss thrives on damp soil, whether the area is sunny or shady. Beetles like to lay their eggs in damp soil, and fungal diseases thrive in places where it's wet. To avoid these problems, don't water more frequently than every four to six days.

Additionally, if lawns are watered for fifteen or twenty minutes at a time the grass will have shallow roots. A short root system is more prone to heat damage in very hot weather, winterkill, and grub injury. If an irrigation system delivers water over a longer period and the soil is dampened six or more inches down, plants are stronger and the soil surface can dry up without injury to the lawn.

Although people ask for a specific length of time to run their irrigation, this is impossible to give since every system is different. The amount of water that's delivered will vary from house to house because of differences in water pressure and sprinkler heads. In general, a lawn needs about three quarters of an inch of water every seven days, as measured in a rain gauge. So setting a rain gauge, not a carton or tuna can, on the lawn and running the sprinklers until it shows three quarters of an inch is the only way to determine how long your system should be on.

Whenever possible, be sure any automatic system has the ability to measure when it has rained or is raining, so that water won't be wasted or applied unnecessarily. Better yet, if you're able to monitor rain in your gauge, keep the lawn irrigation set on "manual" and turn it on only when needed.

At the end of the summer it's easy to see which parts of a lawn are in full sun and which areas are shaded. Even if a lawn is being watered, the heat of the direct sun can dry open areas.

MOWING LAWNS Grass should be cut to three inches high or higher. Longer blades mean more leaf surface for photosynthesizing, which grows stronger plants. Long grass also shades the soil surface better, which minimizes the germination of weed seeds and prevents the soil from drying as quickly. Let grass clippings fall so that they add their nutrients back into the soil.

WEED MANAGEMENT When a lawn is filled with weeds that can be a sign that the overall health of the turf needs addressing. Compact soil does not support good grass growth, for example, but weeds such as plantain thrive in compact areas. Nut sedge (aka nut grass) loves wet soils, so its presence often shows that a lawn is being kept too moist. Sorrel is an indicator weed for acidic soils and crabgrass thrives in hot, dry spaces where the normal turf grasses have failed.

If you're looking for a weed-free lawn you'll need constantly address the new weeds as they appear. Removing weeds promptly, before they have a chance to spread, is the best way to keep them out of the lawn. Weeds can be dug out or killed with a broadleaf weed killer.

CRABGRASS Crabgrass is best controlled by applying a pre-emergent herbicide in the spring; this prevents these seeds from germinating. Apply a pre-emergent when the forsythia shrubs flower because that precedes the time when the soil temperature is right for germination. Unfortunately, there is no easy organic pre-emergent. Although corn gluten was thought to have promise for this use, it requires a combination of perfect timing and weather to be effective. Since corn gluten is also a fertilizer, it usually stimulates weed growth instead of preventing the germination of crabgrass.

BENTGRASS If you've looked out on your lawn in the morning and seen patches of grass that are lighter in color, you've probably got creeping bentgrass (*Agrostis palustris*). This grass is purposefully used on golf courses where it is mowed very low, but when it seeds in home lawns it's a completely different color and texture than our regular turf. It can also look messy because of the way it grows in tufts of blades on sprawling, brown and bending stems.

Since bentgrass loves moisture, it's more likely to infest home lawns that are watered too frequently. When patches of this plant are small it's fastest to dig them out, add new loam, and reseed. Larger patches might have to be killed with herbicide, and most herbicides will also kill your lawn. Whether you dig it out or kill it in place, watch carefully for small plants that return from seeds that are in your soil. After new lawn has been established where the bentgrass grew, change watering so that the surface of your lawn isn't so damp.

GRUBS Most people are far more afraid of grub damage than they need to be. With the proper lawn care grubs damage doesn't occur frequently. If lawns are watered deeply less often, beetles are less attracted to laying eggs in the turf. Additionally, the longer roots created by deep soakings can withstand some grub feeding without as much damage. Finally, applying

Bentgrass is a lighter color and finer texture than common lawn grasses. Catch it when the patches are small so that it's easier to dig out.

insecticides regularly can actually kill off beneficial predators and put your lawn's ecosystem out of balance.

The test to see if your lawn has a grub problem is simple: cut a square foot of turf in the area you think is being damaged, and roll up the grass. If you see more than ten grubs there, you have an over-population and might want to treat your turf. But if you only see a few grubs it's probably not worth treating.

The two organic treatments for grubs are milky spore disease and beneficial nematodes. Some lawn experts recommend using both if your grub population is significant in that milky spore takes a few years to build up effective control while the nematodes provide more immediate help. Follow the instructions on the packages for the proper application.

Moss The myth is that moss in a lawn means you need to add lime. If getting rid of moss only meant raising pH, no one would have moss in their lawn. Although maintaining a near-neutral pH is advisable for growing a healthy lawn, liming is not the answer for moss control. The three things that promote moss growth are too frequent watering, compact soil, and shade. Even if you use a moss killer, if you're watering too often, have compact soil or little sunlight the moss will quickly return. To get rid of moss, alter how you water, aerate your lawn and top-dress with compost to ease compaction.

If shade is the issue, limb-up or remove trees to allow more sunlight to reach the turf, or consider that moss might be the better plant for the job. Moss will thrive without much care and you don't have to mow it. But if you've got your heart set on grass in a shady yard, try seeding every April with a shade-mix. Mow the grass high, to keep it stronger, and water no more frequently than every five days.

LAWN ALTERNATIVES

When I moved to the Cape in the early 1990's I saw several properties that had what was called a "Cape Cod Lawn." This was a surface of pine needles, some weeds that were kept mowed, and occasional patches of the native *Carex pensylvanica*. Although this is fairly low-maintenance, it is not a no-maintenance solution because weeds do appear and the *Carex* is most successful in part shade.

Although perennials and shrubs don't have to be mowed, they actually require more maintenance because of the weeding. Weeds will grow in between, around and even in clumps of perennials; once established such weeds are difficult to remove since their roots are entangled with the other plants' root systems.

Groundcovers are a possibility as a lawn alternative but will need attention for several years while maturing. (See Chapter 7). Even the most weed-smothering plants will need weeds pulled when they are young, and there is always the need for continual removal of vines such as bittersweet. Additionally, although some low perennials such as thyme will tolerate light foot traffic, any regular pressure will kill most perennial plants.

Instead of a front lawn the Spitlers planted a range of perennials and shrubs in front of their Nantucket house.

Pests, Problems, & Treatments
Common insects, diseases, and environmental challenges, and how what we do in our yards and gardens can create healthy, beautiful landscapes.

Chapter 16 *Diseases*

WHEN A PLANT ISN'T DOING WELL it's important to get an accurate diagnosis before any treatment is started. Applying an insecticide to a plant that really has a fungal problem, or using a fungicide on a plant that's actually been physically damaged, is a waste of time and money, and puts substances into the environment needlessly. Using any product in the garden unnecessarily should be avoided because even organic treatments have consequences.

Plant problems can be brought to the Cape Cod Cooperative Extension for analysis, or sent to the diagnostic labs at UMass Amherst. Note that there is a fee for sending samples to the University Extension for identification.

There are three types of diseases that plants can get: fungal, bacterial, and viral. Of these three the most common are diseases caused by fungi. Some fungal problems cause spots or mold on leaves while others rot roots or make a stem's vascular system collapse. Some fungal infections are cosmetic in nature and don't need to be treated. Others can be suppressed with fungicides, and a few don't respond to treatment and can kill plants.

Since there are many fungi that are either benign or beneficial, fungicides should never be applied unless absolutely needed. Additionally, every attempt should be made to be sure that the problem is fungal in origin. Once an accurate diagnosis is made plants can be treated with a fungicide labeled for that particular plant or problem, and used according to directions.

There are several organic fungicides available including those based on sulfur or beneficial bacteria. These should be tried first and they often prevent the situation from getting worse. Although copper-based fungicides are labeled for organic gardening, they should be used sparingly because copper can build up in the soil and it's highly toxic to aquatic life.

Since many fungal problems are either caused or made worse by the frequent splashing of water on foliage, be sure to alter irrigation systems that have been set to go off too frequently. If plants continue to be splashed with water the problem won't be suppressed no matter which type of fungicide is used.

Plants that are prone to fungal problems every year are best treated prophylactically. Begin spraying with an organic fungicide early in the season, *before* the plant begins to show symptoms. Apply the product regularly, according to directions.

LEAF SPOT The most common fungal situation seen on the Cape is leaf spot, which is caused by a large variety of fungi. Leaf spot shows as brown or yellow spots on the foliage that can be small and hard to see, or large enough to mar the appearance of a plant. Sometimes the dead tissue drops out of infected leaves, creating holes that resemble insect damage. Before assuming that leaves are being eaten, look for spots where the tissue has not yet fallen away. Cherry and skip laurels are especially prone to "shot hole fungus" when the foliage is repeatedly splashed with water.

It is common to see leaf spots on rhododendrons in the early spring. People get concerned because the leaves are either yellow or are yellowing at that time. The spots are fungal damage that happened the year before. The yellowing leaves are either the old foliage the plant is shedding in preparation for making new growth, or are pale from winter damage. Some varieties are more prone to winter yellowing than others. In either case, the leaf spot is seldom a matter for concern.

POWDERY MILDEW Some plants are prone to this fungus, which creates a grey or silver powder-like substance on leaves and stems. In ornamentals, mildew might disfigure the plants but seldom kills them. Powdery mildew on lilacs, for example, doesn't need to be treated. Perennials that are prone to this fungal infection include summer Phlox (*Phlox paniculata*) bee balm (*Monarda*), and peonies (*Paeonia*). All of these can be cut to the ground as flowering wanes, and the infected stems either put in a brush pile or buried; do not put infected stems or leaves in the compost.

Roses and all types of squash should be sprayed with an organic fungicide starting early in the season. Spray both sides of leaves and the stems to slow the progression of the disease so that the full season of blooms or vegetables is possible.

DOWNY MILDEW Downy mildews are water molds, and the two plants that are prone to damage are regular impatiens (*Impatiens walleriana*) and basil (*Ocimum basilicum*). Downy mildew isn't a problem that will go away over time, but some years are worse than others. If you want to grow impatiens or basil, it's important to know how to work with and around the problem.

Impatiens downy mildew (*Plasmopara obducens*) is active in cool, damp conditions. So planting impatiens too early in the season makes it more vulnerable to infection, and automatic sprinklers that go off at night or very early morning can also contribute. Set sprinklers to go off after sunrise and water deeply every four or five days instead of more frequently. In a dry

While powdery mildew is seen on the tops of leaves, evidence of downy mildew shows most underneath foliage. Basil plants infected with downy mildew typically show yellowing foliage sometime in July.

summer your impatiens might be fine all season but begin to defoliate once cool, damp weather arrives in fall. If desired, spray weekly with a fungicide labeled as being effective on downy mildew; this isn't a cure, but a way to slow the disease and keep plants looking good into early fall.

New Guinea impatiens and Sunpatiens are resistant to downy mildew so these don't need to be treated. Flower breeders have been developing types of *Impatiens walleriana* that are resistant to downy mildew, and the first ones will begin to be sold in 2019.

Basil downy mildew (*Peronospora belbahrii*) is different from impatiens downy mildew. This disease causes yellowing leaves and plant death in mid to late summer. The lower leaves start to yellow first, and a gray sporulation is visible on the underside of the leaves, especially in the early morning.

Management of basil downy mildew includes spraying with one of the bio-fungicides (*Bacillus amyloliquefaciens*, *B. subtilis*, or *Streptomyces lydicus*) every ten days to two weeks from planting onward. Since these are the same fungicides that can be used to control early blight on tomatoes and powdery mildew on squash, vegetable gardeners can use the product of their choice on all these plants.

Eventually, however, basil plants will start to show signs of downy mildew. Once the lower leaves start to show symptoms, the top two-thirds of the plant can be cut and the leaves made into pesto. Fortunately, downy mildew is edible and pesto can be frozen in small patties and used as needed. If the bottom parts of the basil plants continue to be treated with the fungicide, the plants often rebound with some fresh growth that can be harvested until frost.

Spice, lemon, lime and the purple basils are resistant to downy mildew and can be used the same way as the Italian sweet basil in cooking. New cultivars of basil that are resistant to downy mildew such as Amazal, from Proven Winners, are being released, so watch for these plants. African blue basil (*Ocimum kilimandscharicum* × *basilicum* 'Dark Opal') is not only impervious to downy mildew but because the flowers are sterile the flowers don't have to be pinched. The flavor of African blue basil has a strong, camphor-scented quality but it's still useful for cooking. This basil is very attractive in the garden and the bees love it.

BLACK KNOT Wild cherry trees and cultivated plums and cherries are prone to getting black knot (*Apiosporina morbosa*) a fungus that causes bumpy black areas on trunks and stems. Some trees live with this disease for years while others will die back as twigs and branches become girdled. Small infestations should be removed, cutting about three inches below the black growth. Throw infected cuttings away since they may still contain spores. For valuable trees, a copper or sulfur fungicide can be sprayed just before bud break and regularly after that according to directions. Although this won't cure an infected tree it can slow the disease down.

BOTRYTIS This disease is also known as gray mold. There are several types of botrytis and plants that are commonly affected include peonies (*Peonia*), annual geraniums (*Pelargonium*) and ninebark (*Physocarpus*). Cool damp weather tends to promote this disease and watering too frequently makes it worse. Symptoms of peony botrytis include blackened buds that don't develop, stems that turn dark and collapse, and flowers that brown quickly. Use a fungicide labeled for the problem if needed, spraying the plant before signs of botrytis are seen.

SOOTY MOLD If you notice that your holly, yew or other plants have a charcoal gray coating over the leaves, you've probably got sooty mold. This is a collective term for several different fungi that grow where sugar-rich plant juices have been deposited. The problem stems from an infestation of an insect with sucking mouthparts, such as aphids, scale, or whitefly. These insects excrete plant juices that are high in sugars, which support the growth of several types of fungi. Although sooty mold isn't good for the foliage of plants, the real issue is the insects that cause it. Spray plants that have sooty mold with horticultural oil, making sure to coat the stems and under the leaves. Repeat this treatment as the label directs.

BACTERIAL DISEASES Although these diseases aren't nearly as common as fungal problems, there are a few bacterial problems that occur on the Cape and Islands. Lilac blight, which turns foliage and stems black, is one that many notice. Cherry and plum trees are frequently killed by bacterial canker, and fire blight is occasionally seen on *Pyracantha*. The lumpy crown gall that can occur at the bottom of *Euonymus* plants is also bacterial in origin. Although some bacterial diseases can be treated with a copper-based fungicide, in most cases it doesn't save the plant once the bacteria has taken hold. When clipping off damaged stems and other parts of plants you suspect have a bacteria-caused problem, dip your pruners into a bleach and water solution after every cut to minimize spreading the disease.

VIRAL DISEASES Plants that have a virus often grow distorted yellow foliage. Although they are not common, viruses do occasionally kill plants. Since there is no cure for a virus in plants it's probably not necessary to send a sample to the lab at the University of Massachusetts Extension service, but this is a possibility if a definitive identification is desired.

DISEASE LOOK-ALIKES The overuse of herbicides can look like a virus or other plant disease. Too much weed killer can cause stunted, deformed growth. Plants that have been given too much of a single element, such as boron or magnesium (Epson salt) can also look as if a disease is present. Before concluding that your plant has a fungal, bacterial or viral problem, think about what substances might have been applied to the soil in the area.

Leaf damage can also be a result of something making contact with the foliage. Cleaning solutions from power-washing houses or decks, salt from

They look like alien lobsters emerging from the ground, but these are a form of stinkhorn fungus. Stinking or stinky squid (Pseudocolus fusiformis) *might smell like rotten meat, but they are harmless and short-lived.*

winter roads, and even sun-heated water from a garden hose can kill or distort leaves and stems. Before you assume that a disease is the cause of plant problems, think back to what has happened around that plant in recent weeks.

MUSHROOMS, STINKHORNS, GHOST PLANTS & SLIME MOLDS

There are several fungi and slime molds that pop up, often causing people to worry. All usually appear following a rainy period on decaying organic matter such as mulch. Mushrooms come in assorted shapes, colors and sizes. Usually they come and go quickly and aren't cause for concern. If you think a child or dog might be attracted to them, shovel or rake them up, but otherwise they can be ignored.

Stinkhorn fungi arrive in a variety of impressive shapes and they smell like dead animals. Because of the rotting carrion odor they attract flies and beetles which spread their spores to other areas. Again, these are nothing to worry about, but if the odor bothers you, shovel them up or pluck them out of the soil with gloves on, and throw them into the woods or garbage.

Ghost plants (*Monotropa uniflora*) are also called Indian pipe. These pure white plants grow about six inches high and are interesting because they are not a fungus but a plant that does not make chlorophyll. These are usually found growing in the woods because they get their energy from the mycorrhizal fungi that grow with tree roots. So ultimately, these ghostly perennials depend on the energy that the trees are producing. Leave them where they grow since they do no harm.

Slime molds look like an alien has vomited in the garden. They appear overnight and are yellow, orange or tan in color. Some call them "dog vomit fungus." Within three or four days they turn black and are gone, and other than possibly smothering very young seedlings they do no harm. Turn them into the earth with a shovel or wash away with a jet of water.

These "dog vomit" slime molds can be pale tan, rusty brown or brilliant yellow. They come and go quickly, and do no harm.

Many mistake the fuzzy lichen that we see growing on the branches of trees and shrubs as something harmful. While the presence of lichen can indicate a plant that is weaker, the lichen itself does not harm trees or shrubs.

Chapter 17
Animals, Unwanted & Wanted

ANIMAL DIFFICULTIES Gardeners deal with critters that cause damage, and want to know how to attract the ones that are cute or colorful. Rabbits, crows, woodchucks, deer, moles, skunks, voles, turkeys, geese, rats and chipmunks can all drive homeowners crazy because of the damage they do or the excrement they leave behind. Yet while we'd like to discourage those animals, there are pretty birds that we want to attract. This chapter deals with deterring and enticing wildlife.

Wild turkeys can cause some damage as they scratch and peck, looking for food, but fortunately they usually move on as long as no one is feeding them. Do not feed wild turkeys because they can become very territorial about the person who feeds them and aggressive toward others.

Many of our problems with destructive animals stem from our own actions. As wild areas continue to be developed, critters have no choice but to share our yards and gardens. And when we fail to respect predators such as coyotes, and remove places where foxes can live and raise young, the populations of smaller animals that they live on are allowed to increase unchecked. Even skunks, an animal that most people think is a nuisance, are predators that eat baby rodents. So part of dealing with critter problems is to provide for and protect predators.

Another key to coping with animal damage is patience. Animal populations rise and fall, and what seems to be a plague of voles or chipmunks one year won't necessarily be as large in coming seasons. And even in a single summer animals might damage the landscape for a period of time, but then move on to other areas and not be a problem again. Beyond maintaining a certain level of tolerance, however, there are ways to keep animal damage to a minimum.

Before taking any sort of action, make sure you have accurately identified the animal that is damaging your plants or property. For example, many people blame moles for eating the roots of their plants when this small animal is not to blame. Moles are carnivores and eat grubs, worms and insects, while voles are herbivores that live on roots and stems. So looking for a treatment for moles when voles are the problem will be a waste of time.

Here is a quick guide to help you identify which critter is responsible for what you see. If the tops of plants are eaten but the lower stems remain, it's likely to be deer. A stand of *Hosta* that has leaves missing while the stems remain, or a perennial that has been grazed so it's down to two feet tall, is typical of deer damage. Rabbits eat leaves as well, but often do so from the top up, especially on taller plants. Woodchucks eat the plants right down to the ground, stems and all.

Lawns are torn up by moles, crows and skunks, who are eating grubs. Usually this damage is finite, and stops once their food source is all consumed. It's silly to treat for grubs at this point because the moles, crows or skunks have already removed them. Patch the lawn and forget about it.

Squirrels and chipmunks usually eat seeds but they will also devour leaves in the early spring. Squirrels will snap off tulip heads, not to eat the flowers as the deer do, but to drink the water that flows up the stem. Similarly, chipmunks will eat on low-growing tomatoes because they are thirsty. Turkeys eat seeds and insects, but can do damage by trampling plants. They and the geese also generate a great deal of bird poop, which can be annoying when it's all over your deck or patio.

No matter which critter is causing the problem, there are five ways to deal with them beyond killing them. You will note that I do not suggest trapping problematic critters and moving them elsewhere. For several good reasons, it is illegal to do so in the state of Massachusetts. Homeowners or pest control companies can certainly trap animals, but after doing so will need to kill them, not release them in other areas.

Many people have trouble with deer and rabbits eating their Hosta *in shade gardens.* Hellebores *are a good shade plant that Bambi and Thumper won't eat.*

BREAK THEIR HABITS Animals are creatures of habit. If they find a tasty food source they will return to that area again and again to feed. This is wonderful if it's an animal we love, such as a hummingbird, but less appealing when a bunny eats up the annuals we've spent time planting. Knowing that animals can get into a routine is in our favor, however. Sometimes if you can break their customs with the use of physical barriers or repellants, your nemesis will go on to other patterns in other areas.

PHYSICAL BARRIERS There are many ways to physically block animals from getting to your plants. Nets or cages can be used to cover blueberry bushes or vegetables for example, or gardens fenced to keep out rabbits. Floating row cover, a non-woven, lightweight fabric that is sold at garden centers, can be draped over vegetables to prevent animals from getting to the crops before you do. Row cover needs to be held down with logs, pins or stones to prevent it from blowing away. Sometimes covering plants when they are small is enough, and the row cover can be removed once the plants are taller and less tender or tasty.

Woodchucks and other pest animals frequently live under sheds or porches, so the first step in animal control should be to block these areas with fencing. Never leave a space where an animal can get under a shed or porch. Bury a good foot of the fencing sloping out, away from the shed or porch, so that animals are discouraged from digging under, and staple the fencing to the shed or bottom of the deck. The wire can be covered with lattice if desired.

SCARE THEM OFF One of the best ways to scare animals is with a motion-activated sprinkler. Two that I have used and had success with are the Spray Away by Havahart and the Scarecrow by Contech. These are

The fence around Melissa Caughey's garden in Osterville kept small animals out of her vegetables.

attached to a garden hose and when the motion sensor detects animals, the sprinkler opens and lets out a sudden and strong blast of water. These sprinklers can be adjusted to detect small or large animals. They are effective in repelling deer, crows, rabbits, cats, woodchucks, raccoons, turkeys, skunks and squirrels. These are also effective against two-legged pests who might be stealing your hydrangea flowers or picking your peonies.

Many animals can be scared away by replicas of predators. Fake owls and hawks can deter other birds. Large rubber snakes placed on a roof can be effective at keeping flickers or other woodpeckers from drumming on houses, and plastic coyotes can help keep geese off lawns. All of these man-made predators should be moved around frequently, however, because if they remain in one place too long all the wildlife gets used to them and learns that they aren't really a threat.

Another product that's very effective in scaring off deer is the Wireless Deer Fence. This battery-operated wand was developed using the same principle that farmers have used for years by baiting their electric fences with peanut butter. The deer are attracted to the scent of the peanut butter but then get a shock from the fence; because a deer has a flight response, it bolts from the fence and doesn't come back. The Wireless Deer Fence holds a scent tube that is set in between short prongs that deliver a shock when a deer sniffs it. You charge up the wand and start the season by putting it near plants that the deer typically are drawn to, such as hosta and daylilies. As the summer goes along, the wands can be moved to any plant that shows deer grazing, and the damage will stop. This product is available only online and just works for deer; it isn't effective for rabbits or woodchucks.

Repellants Let's start with what not to do: do not use mothballs. These are poison, and have no place in the garden, under a shed, or in the lawn. Do not use chewing gum because this "remedy" is an old myth that is completely ineffective. Do not use random kitchen products, or items from under the bathroom sink. Finally, I'm also opposed to fox or coyote urine because these are collected in a very inhumane manner. That said, repellants can be quite effective as long as they are targeted to specific animals and applied frequently.

You can make your own rabbit and deer repellant by combining one cup of milk and one beaten egg into one half-gallon of water. Strain the mixture through a dishcloth to remove egg solids before putting it into a sprayer. This is an effective rabbit and deer repellant because they are herbivores, but it should only be sprayed on ornamental plants, not edibles.

Blood-based repellants are also effective for rabbits and deer, so many commercial animal repellants contain blood. Blood meal can be sprinkled in a garden although it can be less effective since it doesn't stick on the plants. Another repellant that is often sprinkled in gardens to repel Bambi and Thumper is Milorganite, the fertilizer made from Milwaukee sewer sludge. Although Milorganite can be effective, it shouldn't be used too frequently because too much nitrogen and the other nutrients aren't good for plants.

Other repellants often contain herb oils, garlic or hot peppers. These can be useful to get critters to break their habits and move on. Hot pepper mixes, including cayenne pepper powder, or liquid scotch bonnet peppers in water with some Turbo, a spreader-sticker product available at garden centers, in the sprayer, can keep squirrels and chipmunks away from newly-planted bulbs, flowers and new spring foliage.

Many gardeners experiment with grinding mints, garlic or peppers in a blender, letting the mixture sit for a couple of hours and then straining the brew through a dishtowel into a sprayer. A teaspoon or two of Turbo can help these concoctions stick on the plants. Although they aren't always 100% effective, such repellants can often break an animal's habits well enough to persuade the critter to move on.

TRAP CROPS Offering animals an alternative to your garden plants can sometimes mean the difference between accepting minimal damage and all out war. The best example of this is rabbits and white clover. Although bunnies will occasionally nibble on some of my plants, most of the time they prefer the clover that grows in my lawn. I'll spray the plants I know they like with a repellant, and let them feast on the clover. Woodchucks prefer plantain (*Plantago major*), so a smart gardener allows that broadleaf weed to flourish in areas that are a distance away from vegetables.

Another approach is to intermingle plants that are preferred by critters with those that aren't so appealing. This is not only a practical method but one that fits right in with current trends in garden design. More and more gardens are being planted in plant communities that resemble how nature grows plants. In this style, two or three annual or perennial plants are combined in and among each other instead of being planted in exclusive clusters. Think of how a field looks, or the tapestry of moss, wintergreen and Mayflower on the floor of a Cape Cod woodland, and plant accordingly.

ATTRACTING WILDLIFE The opposite side of dealing with animal damage is attracting beautiful birds, butterflies, and other wildlife to the garden. There are four main ways to make your property into a habitat that's desirable to animals. The first is to have a wide diversity of plantings that includes many native species. For example, many people don't realize that the oaks and wild cherry trees support a wide range of wildlife, so leaving those plants in a yard is extremely important.

Secondly, a wide variety of plants and planting styles provides a range of food and sheltering places. Plant things that are known food sources such as American holly (*Ilex opaca*), winterberry (*Ilex verticillata*), red cedar (*Juniperus virginiana*), elderberry (*Sambucus canadensis*) and switchgrass (*Panicum virgatum*). Grow some plants in thickly-planted groups for nesting and hiding places.

Third, have a source of fresh water available such as a birdbath or shallow water feature. And finally, keep all pesticides to a minimum so that you're not killing beneficial insects and predators. Remember that everything is connected to everything else.

When many people talk about attracting wildlife, they are often thinking about birds. To bring birds to your property you can supply food and fresh water, but a diverse selection of plants is also important. Most Agastache *and* Salvia *flowers attract hummingbirds, no matter what color the blooms are.*

Chapter 18 *Insects*

SOME OF THE INSECT PROBLEMS in this region are very host-specific, and in these cases I might have mentioned them in the section where I talk about that particular plant. Chilli thrips, for example, are discussed in the chapter on hydrangeas, the shrub they damage in this region. Others are listed here, whether they attack specific plants or not.

Insect problems can often be moderated or prevented by the presence of natural predators, and these are encouraged by diverse plantings. In other words, the greater the variety of flowers and plants in your yard, the better off you are.

Before treating any insect problem, decide if the amount of damage warrants your intervention. Most insecticides, even those that are organic, kill beneficial insects as well as those that are causing injury to your plants. If there are only a few insects, or if the damage is minor, consider doing nothing. Secondly, determine if what you see is still going on; sometimes we notice holes or other symptoms long after the pest has come and gone. Finally, use the least toxic response to the problem.

ANDROMEDA LACEBUG This tiny insect targets *Pieris japonica*, which is commonly called Andromeda or the lily-of-the-valley shrub. Plants that are placed in sunny locations are more prone to lacebug since they are already under stress. While the new leaves will be solid green, the older foliage of an infested plant will have tiny yellow dots all over them, giving the green a stippled look. Spray spring, summer and fall with horticultural oil, applying it to the underside of the leaves.

APHIDS Aphids are very small and come in a variety of colors. You may see greenish aphids on your roses, orange on the butterfly weed, or black ones on nasturtiums or beans. Although they can distort new foliage or flower buds by piercing the tissues with their sucking mouthparts, aphids seldom do major damage to landscape plants. They can be smashed with your fingers or smothered with insecticidal soap or horticultural oil if their populations are unusually large. When aphids are left alone the predators usually kick in and feed on large populations.

Sometimes you'll see ants surrounding aphids; they are feeding on the sugar-rich "honeydew" that aphids excrete. Ants can even farm aphids by protecting them for their own purposes. If you treat the aphids with oil or insecticidal soap, the ants will go away.

BRONZE BIRCH BORER The larvae of this pest tunnel through the trunks and stems of birch trees, ultimately girdling the plant and causing it to die. In this region it's most active on white birches but not as much on Heritage river birch (*Betula nigra* 'Heritage'). This is a pest that can only survive in weakened trees, so the best prevention is to water birch trees deeply once a week in times of drought, and only prune in the late fall or winter.

CABBAGE LOOPERS If you see holes in the leaves of your kale, cabbage, broccoli, Brussels sprouts and other cole crops, you've probably got cabbage loopers feasting on the foliage. These are the larval form of the white cabbage butterflies. Spray your plants with either Bt or spinosad, adding a spreader-sticker such as Turbo to the sprayer so the product sticks on the plants. Apply every two weeks through the summer.

COLORADO POTATO BEETLES Also called the ten-striped beetle, these insects feed on potatoes, tomatoes, eggplants and peppers, which are all members of the *Solanaceae* family. Although the adult beetles are yellow with dark stripes, the larvae are orange with black dots and the eggs are bright orange. Handpick any of these and smash them, or spray with spinosad or *Beauveria bassiana* fungus.

CUCUMBER BEETLES These small insects have yellow and black stripes on their bodies and black heads. They feed on squash or cucumber plants, weakening them and spreading a bacterial wilt disease that makes the plants collapse almost overnight. Although there isn't a great organic control of these beetles, you can protect young plants with diatomaceous earth sprinkled over stems, leaves and the ground, and knock populations down by spraying with spinosad. The cucumber called County Fair is the most bacterial wilt-resistant variety.

EARWIGS Most people don't like to hear this, but earwigs are beneficial insects. Yes, they look creepy and early in the summer they can do significant damage to some plants. But earwigs eat other pests including aphids, mites and slug eggs, and they consume decaying plants, helping the organic matter to break down into the soil. Early in the season, however, when there is

Dahlias and butterfly bush are two earwig favorites. Dust newly-planted or emerging plants with diatomaceous earth early in order to prevent damage.

less for earwigs to consume, they can strip newly-planted annuals such as coleus and dahlias, and turn butterfly bush foliage into a ragged mess.

Earwigs feed at night and hide in cool, damp places during the day. This makes them easy to trap by rolling up wet newspapers into tubes and securing these rolls with rubber bands or tape. Place the tubes in the garden in the evening so the earwigs crawl in to hide in the early morning, and gather them up the next day for disposal.

To prevent earwigs from stripping newly-planted annuals and perennials, dust with diatomaceous earth immediately after planting. Usually one light application to foliage and the ground immediately around the young plant is sufficient.

FLEA BEETLES These tiny black insects eat small holes in new vegetables. Dust the plants and surrounding soil with diatomaceous earth once or twice when the new growth is tender. Usually this takes care of the problem.

FOUR-LINED PLANT BUG If you see groups of perfectly round, tan or gray spots on annual or perennial plants in early July, it's likely that you have the four-lined plant bug. They are particularly drawn to Russian sage, oregano, mums, mint and other herbs. The good news about this insect is that there is just one generation per summer and the damage is mostly cosmetic. You can knock back large populations with insecticidal soap, neem, diatomaceous earth, or horticultural oil. Clip off leaves that are especially damaged to stimulate new growth.

GYPSY MOTH Gypsy moth larvae have periodically done great damage to trees on the Cape and Islands. When the spring is damp these larvae are controlled by a fungus, *Entomophaga maimaiga*. The fungus is activated in wet weather and the caterpillars are infected when they crawl across the

This photo shows female gypsy moths laying eggs on a tree. The rusty-colored eggs can be sprayed with horticultural oil to smother some of them, but scraping them off the bark won't help as they will hatch anyway.

damp ground and pick up the spores. If you see the carcasses of dead caterpillars hanging shriveled on the trunks of trees, you'll know the fungus killed them. Leave the dead bodies on the trees, because these are filled with fungus spores which will be dispersed to the ground for the future.

If populations of gypsy moth larvae build again, spraying your most vulnerable trees with spinosad when the caterpillars are small will protect those plants. Do not spray plants where bees are foraging, however, as wet spinosad is not good for bees. Once this bacteria is dry it doesn't harm pollinators, but it shouldn't be used on plants in flower.

HEMLOCK WOOLY ADELGID This insect looks like tiny pieces of cotton clustered on the stems, and can be seen on hemlocks in the fall and spring. If untreated, most hemlocks will become thin and die within a few years. Spray annually with horticultural oil in spring and fall. There are also systemic insecticides that are effective if the trees are treated early enough, but these are the last resort. Most people are no longer planting hemlocks in this area since they need such constant protection from the adelgid.

HIBISCUS SAWFLY LARVAE This is a tiny green worm that very quickly turns hardy hibiscus leaves into lace. Spray the underside of your plants with spinosad or Bt in late June to control this larvae. Usually one application is enough.

JAPANESE & ASIAN GARDEN BEETLES Both beetles eat foliage and are most active at night. Japanese beetles are shiny, metallic black and Asian garden beetles are brown. One method of control is to hand-knock them into a carton filled with an inch of cooking oil, doing this in the early morning or evening when they are most visible. Spraying the plants with a product containing *Beauveria bassiana*, an entomopathogenic fungus, can also help although this treatment might not be easily found.

Grubs are the larval form of these beetles, so treating lawns with milky spore and/or beneficial nematodes can help keep populations down. Finally, watering your lawn deeply but less often can help; beetles look for moist soil to lay their eggs, so a lawn that's watered frequently attracts more beetles to your property.

In order for beetle traps to be successful they need to be placed some distance away from your garden. These traps use pheromones to attract the beetles, so they ultimately attract more beetles to the area than are caught. If placed in your landscape they will bring more beetles into your yard than they trap.

Lily leaf beetle This bright red beetle eats the foliage of true lilies, but not daylilies. It is the larvae that do the most damage, however, and many people don't pay any attention to them because they look like flecks of mud. In fact, the larvae have the charming habit of piling their own excrement on their backs to hide themselves. The best control is to knock adult beetles into a carton of cooking oil, and spray the plants with spinosad to kill the larvae.

Mexican bean beetles The larvae of these insects are bright yellow or orange, the eggs are yellow and the beetle itself looks like a fat, drab ladybug. This is a pest of bean plants, and is most problematic in community gardens where there are many plants to feed on. Control by smashing adults, larvae and eggs by hand, spraying with spinosad, or applying a product containing *Beauveria bassiana* fungus to the plants and ground. Remove all old plants at the end of the season and till soil in the fall to expose the pupae to freezing temperatures.

Mites Although spider mites are commonly thought of as pests of indoor plants, there are mites that can be problematic outdoors as well. The spruce spider mite is the most common on the Cape and Islands, feeding primarily on all types of spruce but also on arborvitae, hemlock, cedar, larch, juniper, and pine plants. The needles of a plant under attack become very lightly stippled. This is a cool-weather mite so apply treatment such as horticultural oil or a miticide in spring and fall.

Twospotted spider mites are active in the heat of the summer. These feed on a very wide variety of plants including hydrangea, beans and squash. The foliage on plants with significant mite populations will turn pale and stippled. Spray with a miticide according to directions.

Rhododendron borer A rhody with borers might look like it needs water, or is losing limbs because of drought stress. If your leaves on a rhododendron are losing color, curling and dying, check down the length of that stem for holes, sawdust, or evidence of frass (excrement) near the hole or on the ground. Prune off wilted branches and destroy.

Rhododendron lace bug Like the Andromeda lace bug, this insect pierces the leaf and makes rhododendron foliage look yellow and stippled.

The underside of the leaf will look dirty. Spray the underside of the leaves with horticultural oil in May, June and July.

RHODODENDRON ROOT WEEVIL There are a few species of root weevil that attack rhododendrons. The adults eat the edges of the leaves, leaving them notched and raggedy. The larvae eat the shrubs' roots, causing damage that isn't easily seen. The most common means of control is to put burlap or other cloth under the plants and shake them; the beetles drop onto the cloth which can then be gathered and stepped on to smash the insects. Alternatively, beneficial nematodes can be soaked into the soil under and around each plant.

SCALE Scale insects can be round, firm dots, soft white lumps or clumps that look like cotton. Some are so small that the only way you'll know your plant has scale is the presence of a black coating on the plant's leaves. This is the sooty mold that grows on the scale's sugar-rich excrement. Blue hollies are prone to getting scale, as are yews. Most scales are treated with horticultural oil, or a combination of horticultural oil and neem. Repeated applications might be necessary.

SLUGS & SNAILS Slugs and snails love to travel over damp soil, which gives us another reason not to run the irrigation every day. A garden that dries in between soakings will have fewer slugs and snails. Dusting newly-placed plants with diatomaceous earth will prevent them from being skeletonized, and using an iron-based bait such as Sluggo, is also helpful with slug and snail control. Encouraging a diverse wildlife population is also helpful in that toads, snakes, turtles and some beetles and birds make slugs a part of their diet. Yes, the saucers of beer work, but frankly I think that there are better uses for this beverage.

SUNFLOWER MOTH There is a new pest in the area that can damage the attractiveness of *Echinacea* and assorted sunflowers. It's called the sunflower moth larvae (*Homoeosoma electellum*) and the tiny caterpillar eats the center of the cones. Spraying the cones early in the season with spinosad, taking care not to treat when bees are on the flowers, will help control these larvae.

SQUASH BUGS These insects are grey and shield-shaped. They are easy to catch and squish with gloved hands, and their golden eggs, laid in tight clusters on the underside of squash leaves, are easy to spot and smash as

There are several types of scale. Blue hollies are prone to scale and since it's under the foliage you'll need to spray horticultural oil on the underside of the leaves.

well. Diatomaceous earth, dusted over the stems and soil, can help suppress a large population of squash bugs, and some report some success with neem. When squash plants are young, covering them with floating row cover helps protect them while they grow larger and stronger.

SQUASH VINE BORER These moths lay their eggs on the stems or leaves of squash plants. When the larvae hatch out and tunnel into the stems, they cause the plant to collapse and die from that point outward. There are several ways to control this pest, and sometimes it takes a couple of methods to fend them off. The first is to dust the ground around your young plants, and later the stems themselves, with wood ash or diatomaceous earth. The adult moth doesn't like to crawl through the ashes or DE to lay their eggs. Be aware, however, that repeated applications of wood ash can raise pH in the soil, so at some point you'll have to switch to DE or other methods.

Covering the main stems with mulch is also effective in that the moth can't reach the preferred laying sites. Follow this with spraying either Bt or spinosad on all remaining stems and leaves above the mulch so that any larvae that hatch from eggs laid in these areas will be killed when they start to eat into the stem. Watch for eggs and crush or remove them as they are found; borer eggs are copper to gold in color, small and hard. They are spaced over a stem or leaf while the squash bug eggs are grouped tightly together.

TURPENTINE BEETLE Pitch pine trees (*Pinus rigida*) are the most vulnerable to this pest, although it can also attack Japanese black pine (*P. thunbergii*), Scots pine (*P. sylvestris*), and white pines (*P. strobus*). You will know that your tree has this borer by the pitch tubes that can be seen on the lower part of the trunk. The beetle itself can cause the tree to decline or die, but it also carries a fungus that further weakens infected trees. Unfortunately, when pitch pines break or fall in storms, it attracts the beetles to the area and other trees are more likely to be targeted. There is no good organic treatment for the turpentine beetle, but valuable trees can be protected by applying an insecticide labeled for bark beetles to the lower six feet of the tree's trunk in late April and again in late May, or one month after the first application.

VIBURNUM LEAF BEETLE The first step in controlling damage from this pest is to plant *Viburnum* varieties that are resistant. Fortunately, two of the favorites for the Cape and Islands, Korean spice (*V. carlesii*) and doublefile (*V. plicatum*) are among the most unaffected by the beetle. Plants that show damage from the leaf beetle should be sprayed with horticultural oil in early April before the plants break dormancy, and with spinosad in late April or early May.

WHITEFLY Japanese holly is the plant most commonly infested with whitefly in this region. If you see black, sooty mold on the leaves of your *Ilex crenata*, it's most likely growing on the honeydew that whitefly excretes.

You might also notice swarms of tiny white insects flying out of a Japanese holly shrub when it is shaken. Spray with horticultural oil three or more times during the growing season to suppress this insect.

WINTER MOTH Although the moths fly in early December, it's the larvae that hatch out in the early spring that do damage to shrubs and trees. Winter moth larvae can defoliate maple, birch, apple, beech and cherry foliage. They also attack blueberry flowers and rose leaves, and will occasionally munch on other shrubs or perennials. Spray vulnerable trees that aren't in flower with spinosad as the foliage grows in April and May. Since spinosad isn't good for bees when it's wet, either use Bt on plants that are flowering, or wait until their bloom period is over. Using these methods you'll avoid hitting foraging bees.

Although the winter moth larvae numbers seem to be diminishing in Massachusetts, selected pockets of damage continue. Look at your trees and shrubs closely every week through the spring to see if treatment is needed.

Chapter 19 *Weeds*

People often complain about pokeweed, but these, along with jewelweed, gold-enrod and other native plants, supply food for wildlife. If there are areas of your yard that you can allow such weeds to grow, by all means do.

THERE ARE TWO TYPES of weed problems Cape and Island gardeners face. The first is the group of weeds that pop up in flowerbeds, lawns and vegetable gardens.

Some of these are annuals that germinate every year in the spring, summer or fall, and they are most easily dealt with by hand-pulling or cutting off with a hoe. Controlling perennial weeds requires more work because it's necessary to remove the majority of their roots so that they won't come back. No matter which removal method is used, there isn't a way to permanently ban weeds from a landscape because seeds will remain in the soil only to sprout and grow again. Mother Nature hates bare soil, and whenever possible she'll move some weeds in to cover it, no matter how difficult the growing conditions.

A few of the most difficult weeds we battle are mugwort (*Artemisia vulgaris*), common violets (*Viola sororia*), creeping Charlie (*Glechoma hederacea*), bishop's weed (*Aegopodium podagraria*), Japanese knotweed (*Fallopia japonica*) and creeping bellflower (*Campanula rapunculoides*). Once a property is infested with any of these, serious digging and years of constant attention to the removal of every small sprig will be needed.

Weeds can be best kept at bay by covering as much ground as possible with plants that shade the soil so that weed seeds can't germinate. Mulching bare soil also helps, and the more quickly any and all weeds are removed by hand or hoe, the easier it will be to stay on top of them. In some situations the use of an appropriate weed killer or pre-emergent herbicide might also be employed.

THE JUNGLE CONSTANTLY CREEPS IN The second type of weeds that we need to be aware of in this area is the "bird-planted jungle." These weeds are far more serious in that they are larger, and have the ability to strangle trees and turn a backyard into an impenetrable thorny thicket. Some of the plants that are the most problematic are bittersweet (*Celastrus orbiculatus*), polyantha rose (*Rosa multiflora*), wild grapes (*Vitis sp.*), green brier (*Smilax rotundifolia*), Japanese honeysuckle (*Lonicera japonica*), thorny barberry (*Berberis thunbergii*), and porcelain berry (*Ampelopsis brevipedunculata*). These shrubs and vines are planted by birds when they sit in shrubs and trees and the seeds they've eaten fall to the ground in their excrement.

The challenge of the bird-planted jungle is that the plants above, and others, often escape notice when they are small, but very quickly they overrun shrubs and trees. They kill landscape plants by covering their leaves so that they're denied photosynthesis, or by strangling trunks and branches with their winding vines. Wooded areas and places where landscape plants abut wild spaces should be monitored for such shrubs and vines. At the very least, beating them back annually with a brush cutter or weed whacker

This photo contains four of the thugs that can turn Cape and Island properties into a thorny jungle. The wild blackberry (Rubus sp.) *is easy to spot here because it's in flower. Green brier* (Smilax rotundifolia) *has heart-shaped leaves and thorns on the stems. The wild grape vine* (Vitis vinifera) *has silvery undersides to its leaves, and the bittersweet* (Celastrus orbiculatus) *pokes through in this shot to the left of center.*

is often necessary to prevent them from taking hold. Once these woody weeds are well established, the only remedy is to remove all the vegetation and start again with a blank slate.

OTHER PROBLEM PLANTS In addition to the seeds planted by birds, other plants are so aggressive that whether they were initially grown purposefully in gardens or not, now they have earned the title of "weed." Some of these are on the Massachusetts Prohibited Plant List (https://www.mass. gov/service-details/massachusetts-prohibited-plant-list) meaning that they can no longer be sold in this state. Unfortunately, the horse is out of the barn and these plants pop up faster than we can pull them.

AUTUMN OLIVE (*Elaeagnus umbellata*), with its fragrant flowers and silvery leaf underside is one of the shrubs on this list. Similarly, black locust trees (*Robinia pseudoacacia*) spread rampantly. Both of these are nitrogen-fixing, so they are better able to grow in sand than some desirable plants. Autumn olive seeds are distributed far and wide by birds. Locust trees not only spread from seeds but by suckers that come up from the roots of nearby plants. Once you learn to recognize both plants, watch for seedlings and pull them when they are young. Established plants will need to be cut again and again, or an herbicide applied to their stumps, in order to kill older root systems.

WEED KILLERS Everyone wants an easy, safe way to control weeds, but frankly, it doesn't exist. There are products that can be applied to the soil to prevent weed seeds from germinating, but such pre-emergent herbicides do not kill weeds that are already growing. On the label of such products is a list of plants that the pre-emergent should not be used near, so pay attention to the fine print. Additionally, if a pre-emergent is applied too heavily or too often, the growth of other plants in the area will be stunted or disfigured. Read the label carefully and apply only at the recommended rate.

Although there are broadleaf herbicides that can be spread on lawns to kill weeds but not the grass, the same type of product does not exist for perennials or shrubs. Weed killers that are sprayed onto problem plants will kill everything they touch, and the mist often drifts. Such products should be used sparingly, according to directions.

There are organic weed killers available at garden centers, and although these are often considered less toxic than other synthetic herbicides, they too should be used with caution. Many are made of acetic acid, the active ingredient in vinegar, but the concentration is four or five times greater than the vinegar you purchase in a supermarket. Others are based on cinnamon, clove or other plant oils. Although these organic products are successful for killing foliage, they usually do not kill the roots and so need to be reapplied on perennial weeds and vines such as poison ivy. Some organic herbicides are also toxic to bees and other beneficial insects, so use them carefully and read rates and cautions on the labels. Just because it's labeled "organic" doesn't mean a product is safer or without negative environmental consequences.

Lately there have been many "natural" herbicide recipes that make the rounds online. Most involve supermarket vinegar and Epsom salt. These recipes are not any safer or more effective than commercial organic herbicides, and can, in fact, do *more* damage to soils and surrounding plants. Epsom salt is pure magnesium, and repeated applications of magnesium to a garden can throw off the balance of nutrients and damage plants. Vinegar that is sold for cooking just isn't strong enough to kill plants. You're far better off with an acetic acid-based product from a garden center, used according to directions.

Some weeds can be killed with hot water or a flame. There are torches that attach to a small propane tank that are used to kill weeds. Common sense says that these shouldn't be used on plants growing in mulch or areas where there are dried branches and leaves. You might want a flame to kill the weeds, but you don't want to burn your house down or start a wildfire in the process. Boiling water will cause the top part of a weed to die but doesn't usually get down into the roots. It is most successful on weeds growing in gravel or patio stones, but care must be taken so that the hot water doesn't splash onto your legs or other people.

Chapter 20
Miscellaneous Challenges

SOME PLANT DAMAGE isn't caused by insects or diseases, but by weather or what humans do with and around their plants. These situations are commonly called "cultural conditions" and they can damage or kill plants sometimes more quickly than any bug or fungus. Here are some of the most common cultural conditions that can harm plants.

BURLAP Burlap and wire baskets should always be removed when planting a shrub or tree. If plants are put in the ground with the burlap left in place, it can cause the decline or death of that plant in the years to come.

DROUGHT We can have long periods of drought in this region, and when this happens the root systems of our plants dry up and die back. These reduced root systems can affect plants two or even three years down the

Whenever possible, group plants that are tolerant of dry soils in areas where there is no irrigation. This roadside planting contains orange flowering butterfly weed, yellow yarrow, purple-leafed ninebark shrubs, variegated yucca, asters, 'Morning Light' grasses and daylilies.

road, long after the drought has gone. Sometimes what kills plants is a combination of factors, and extended dry periods can be an important part of the equation. If possible, water plants deeply every week to ten days during a drought. Unless local restrictions prohibit it, use sprinklers or soaker hoses that can drench the entire area under and beyond a plant's canopy.

FERTILIZER BURN When a too-concentrated application of synthetic fertilizer is applied to plants the roots, leaves and stems can brown and die back. This sometimes happens when such fertilizers are used on plants that are dry as well. Always mix fertilizers according to directions and apply to well-hydrated plants. When it comes to fertilizers, more is not better.

HERBICIDE DAMAGE There are a couple of ways that weed killers cause problems on plants. If herbicides are sprayed around valuable plants, the drift can cause anything that is hit to die. You might not even see the spray blowing onto the desirable plants. Secondly, pre-emergent herbicides that are applied repeatedly in the same area, or at a higher concentration than what is recommended, can stunt or distort plants. Similarly, weed killers that are applied to lawns can disfigure or kill plants that are grown nearby.

HOUSEHOLD PRODUCTS Humans are curious animals, and prone to being attracted to the unexpected and quirky. Unfortunately this means that they are likely to reach under the kitchen sink or into the bathroom medicine cabinet for a cure for garden problems. Although some home remedies are safe and might even be effective, many products contain ingredients that can harm plants or put soil chemistry out of whack. For example, plants can be injured by some dish detergents, window cleaners, or Epsom salt. If you see a problem in your landscape, first get an accurate diagnosis, and then use a product that is intended for plants at the rate recommended on the label.

ROPES/CHAINS/TIES When plants lean or fall after a storm, many people tie them up so that they grow straight again. Others stake new plants out of fear that they will tip to one side. Unfortunately, if those supports are left in place, they can strangle and kill plants as the trunks grow. Even the green stretchy ties that are sold in garden centers can kill plants if left wrapped around a stem. If you've tied anything around a plant, even if it seems very loose, make a note on your calendar six months from the installation date to remove all ties.

SALT Whether it's sea-salt laden winds from a hurricane or the drift off roads that are salted in the winter, many plants can be browned or killed if hit by salt. If possible, promptly hose plants off after a hurricane or nor'easter, and place salt-tolerant plants close to any well-traveled road. See the plant list section for suggestions.

TOO MUCH WATER As mentioned several places in this book, irrigation that goes off too frequently is a contributing factor to several plant diseases. Too much water, be it on a lawn, garden beds, or container plants, will cause root rot and other problems. Know that one of the first symptoms of too much water is the same as too little water: the foliage wilts. So if there has been abundant rain or you've watered your landscape frequently, and your plants are drooping, that doesn't necessarily mean that things are thirsty.

Many plants that are being kept too wet develop yellowing leaves. So if the foliage is pale, check the soil around the plant before assuming that the problem is a nutrient deficiency.

WIND/ICE/SNOW BROKEN BRANCHES Homeowners on the Cape and Islands are accustomed to going out after storms and assessing our plants for broken branches, split trunks and cracked limbs. Some storm damage will always be with us in an area where wind, ice and snow are natural occurrences. Whether it's wind that breaks branches or heavy snow that splits a tree's trunk, there usually isn't a good way to repair these wounds that is sustainable long-term.

Plants' branches don't knit back together like human bones do. Yes, you can sometimes bolt a split trunk back together, but since that split never truly mends it will always be a place where moisture will enter and rot the plant from the inside out. Many people have seen a plant that has appeared to have "grown back together," only to have that same branch break off the following winter in heavy snow. Sometimes plants will put out foliage on a cracked or broken branch the first year after the wound since the leaves are running on energy stored in the trunk or limbs; but having used all those resources the first year, such plants frequently die in the second season. Usually the best thing to do when a branch or limb breaks is to make a clean cut and let the plant heal, even if it is no longer the same shape.

Alexander Tureaud's garden in Eastham is a perfect example of how we all need to adapt to changes in the landscape. This yard used to be shaded by trees that came down. Now some of the shade plants still thrive, and new sun-loving plants are being installed. Every gardener needs to be able to be flexible in the face of storm damage and loss of plants for other reasons.

[SECTION IV]

Resources & Community

No matter where you go on the Cape and Islands, there are inspiring plant combinations that make people smile.

Chapter 21
Public Gardens, Nurseries, Education, Horticultural Celebrations, & Plant Lists

The Patchwork Garden at the Long Pond Community Gardens in the town of Barnstable is planted and maintained by volunteers. This group grows cutting flowers that are picked, arranged and distributed every week to random locations where people are in need of a lift. It is just one example of people spreading good will through horticulture on the Cape and Islands.

THE CAPE & ISLANDS are filled with numerous resources for home landscapers and garden lovers. This section contains sources of inspiration, information, plants, and products for Cape and Island garden lovers.

GARDENS OPEN TO THE PUBLIC

Cape Cod

ARMSTRONG-KELLEY PARK – armstrongkelleypark.com
684 Main Street, Osterville

BARNSTABLE FAIRGROUNDS DEMONSTRATION GARDENS
*Planted and maintained by volunteer Master Gardeners, these gardens
are best viewed during the Barnstable County Fair in July.*
1220 Nathan Ellis Highway, Route 151, East Falmouth

CAPE COD MUSEUM OF NATURAL HISTORY – ccmnh.org
Wild flower garden and pollinator path
869 Main Street, Brewster

GREEN BRIAR WILDFLOWER GARDEN – thorntonburgess.org
6 Discovery Hill Road, East Sandwich

HERITAGE MUSEUMS & GARDENS
– heritagemuseumsandgardens.org
67 Grove Street, Sandwich

HIGHFIELD HALL – highfieldhallandgardens.org
56 Highfield Drive, Falmouth

SPOHR GARDENS
45 Fells Pond Road, Falmouth

Martha's Vineyard

POLLY HILL ARBORETUM – pollyhillarboretum.org
809 State Rd, West Tisbury

MYTOI GARDENS
– thetrustees.org/places-to-visit/cape-cod-islands/mytoi.html
41 Dike Road, Edgartown

At Heritage Museums and Gardens in Sandwich there are always beautiful plants in the gardens and something to learn. See mature trees, a wealth of Rhododendrons *and daylilies, and a nationally-known* Hydrangea *test garden.*

Nantucket

HADWEN HOUSE GARDEN
– nha.org/visit/museums-and-tours/hadwen-house
96 Main Street, Nantucket

NURSERIES & GARDEN CENTERS
Cape Cod

AGWAY OF CAPE COD – agwaycapecod.com
20 Lots Hollow Road, Orleans
686 Route 134, South Dennis
1005 Main Street, Chatham

BAYBERRY GARDENS – bayberrygardens.com
250 Route 6, Truro

BRICK KILN FARM – 254brickkilnfarm.com
254 Brick Kiln Road, Teaticket

CAPE COASTAL NURSERY – capecoastalnursery.com
146 Great Western Road, South Dennis

CROCKER NURSERIES – crockernurseries.com
1132 MA-137, Brewster

GREEN RENOVATIONS NURSERY – .gardenrenovationsnursery.com
43 Race Point Road, Provincetown

GREEN SPOT GARDEN CENTER – greenspotgardenctr.com
1085 Route 28, South Yarmouth

HART FARM – hartfarmnursery.com
21 Upper County Road, Dennis Port

HYANNIS COUNTRY GARDEN – hyanniscountrygarden.com
380 West Main Street, Hyannis

MAHONEY'S GARDEN CENTERS – mahoneysgarden.com
958 East Falmouth Hwy, East Falmouth
2929 Falmouth Road, Osterville

PINE TREE NURSERIES – pinetreenursery.com
200 Route 137, South Chatham

SCENIC ROOTS GARDEN CENTER – scenicrootsgardencenter.com
349 MA-6A, East Sandwich

SNOWS GARDEN CENTER – snowscapecod.com
22 Main Street, Orleans

SOARES FLOWER GARDEN NURSERY
 – soaresflowergardennursery.com
1021 Sandwich Road, East Falmouth

SPENCER'S GARDENS & NURSERY
171 Clay Pond Road, Buzzards Bay

THE FARM – thefarmcapecod.com
  40 Rock Harbor Road, Orleans

Martha's Vineyard

DONAROMA'S NURSERY – donaromas.com
  270 Upper Main Street, Edgartown

HEATHER GARDENS – heather-gardens.com
  377 State Road, West Tisbury

JARDIN MAHONEY'S – jardinmahoneymv.com
  45 Edgartown-Vineyard Haven Road, Oak Bluffs

MIDDLETOWN NURSERY & GARDEN CENTER
  – middletownnursery.com
  680 State Road, West Tisbury

VINEYARD GARDENS – vineyardgardens.net
  484 State Road, West Tisbury

Nantucket

ARROWHEAD – arrowheadnursery.com
  9 Wampanoag Way

BARTLETT'S FARM – bartlettsfarm.com
  33 Bartlett Farm Road

PUMPKIN POND FARM – pumpkinpondfarm.com
  25 Millbrook Road

SURFING HYDRANGEA NURSERY – surfinghydrangea.com
  91 Somerset Road

VALERO & SONS INC. GARDEN CENTER – valeroandsons.com
  60 Old South Road, Nantucket

At the Barnstable County Fairgrounds there are demonstration gardens that are open during the fair and normal business hours. See the vegetable garden, herbs, fruit trees, berry bushes and more. The master gardeners of Cape Cod staff the gardens during the fair and are available to answer questions and identify plants.

EDUCATIONAL RESOURCES & HORTICULTURAL CELEBRATIONS

BARNSTABLE COUNTY COOPERATIVE EXTENSION The Cape Cod Extension Service helps homeowners with a wide variety of garden and outdoor situations from deer ticks to diseases of plants. The volunteer master gardeners run an annual series of Backyard Horticulture classes in Harwich and Falmouth that cover lawns, vegetables, flowers, shrubs and more. They have fact sheets on a wide variety of topics that are available online and in their offices. See all of their services at: capecodextension.org/aghort/

CAPE COD HYDRANGEA FESTIVAL This festival honors Cape Cod Gardens of all types. For ten days private gardens are open to the public for the benefit of local non-profits and museums, garden centers and businesses offer special events. Although the event is organized around our signature flower, the Hydrangea, all types of gardens are shown and celebrated. For a complete list of gardens and events – capecodhydrangeafest.com

This lovely firepit and garden was designed by Laura Urban of Urban Design, an interior design firm. It was open during the Cape Cod Hydrangea Festival in 2017 for the benefit of the Harwich Garden Club.

CAPE COD HYDRANGEA SOCIETY The Cape's favorite flower deserves its own organization, and this thriving group meets regularly to provide information and inspiration for hydrangea growers.

– thecapecodhydrangeasociety.org

LOCAL FESTIVALS Several Cape and Island towns celebrate flowers, the coming of spring, harvest or other garden related events. A few of these include the following:

    Brewster: *Brewster In Bloom* – brewster-capecod.com/brewsterblooms/
    Nantucket: *Daffodil Days* – daffodilfestival.com
    Martha's Vineyard: *Living Local Harvest Festival* – livinglocalmv.org
      Grand Illumination – mvcma.org/grand-illumination.html

GARDEN CLUBS There are many garden clubs on the Cape and Islands that meet regularly or hold special events. To find one near you, do an Internet search or ask at your local library for contact information.

GARDEN CONSERVANCY OPEN DAYS Every year several area gardens are open to benefit The Garden Conservancy. For more information check their website – gardenconservancy.org/open-days

UNIVERSITY OF MASSACHUSETTS EXTENSION SERVICE This UMass website provides information about soil testing, weed ID, plant diagnostics and more. Some of these services require a fee, but there is also an abundance of free fact sheets available – ag.umass.edu/services

Bibliography

Armitage, Allan M. *Allen Armitage on Perennials.*
New York: Prentice Hall, 1993.

Del Tredici, Peter. *Wild Urban Plants of the Northeast.*
Ithaca: Cornell University Press, 2010.

Dirr, Michael A. *Hydrangeas for American Gardens.*
Portland: Timber Press, 2004.

Dirr, Michael A. *Manual of Woody Landscape Plants: Their Identification,
Ornamental Characteristics, Culture, Propagation and Uses.*
Champaign: Stipes Publishing, 2009.

DiSabato-Aust, Tracy. *The Well Tended Perennial Garden.*
Portland: Timber Press, 1998.

Fornari, C.L. *A Garden Lover's Cape Cod.*
Beverly: Commonwealth Editions, 2007.

Fornari, C.L. *A Garden Lover's Martha's Vineyard.*
Beverly: Commonwealth Editions, 2008.

Fornari, C.L. *The Cape Cod Garden, Revised.*
Osterville: Paraphyses Press, 2002.

Hudak, Joseph. *Gardening With Perennials Month by Month.*
Portland: Timber Press, 1993.

Nardozzi, Charlie. *New England Month-by-Month Gardening:
What to Do Each Month to Have a Beautiful Garden All Year.*
Minneapolis: Cool Springs Press, 2016.

O'Brien, Greg (ed.). *A Guide to Nature on Cape Cod and the Islands.*
Hyannis: Parnassus Imprints, 1995.

Pell, Susan K., and Bobbi Angell. *A Botanist's Vocabulary.*
Portland: Timber Press, 2016.

Pirone, Pascal P. *Diseases & Pests of Ornamental Plants.*
New York: John Wiley & Sons, Inc., 1978.

Richardson, Mark, and Dan Jaffe. *Native Plants for New England Gardens.*
Guilford: Globe Pequot, 2018.

University of Massachusetts Cooperative Extension System Publications:
Swanson, Deborah C. *Cultural Practices of Woody Plants.*
Clark Roberta A., and Deborah C. Swanson. *Trees for Low Maintenance
Landscapes* – CES Nursery and Landscape Program.

Index

150

million bells (*Calibrachoa sp.*), 37

Milorganite, 144

mint (*Mentha spp.*), 45, 149

Miscanthus sinensis spp. (silver grass) (Japanese silver grass), 59

Miscanthus spp. (grasses), 57

mites, 90–91, 147, 151

mock orange, miniature (*Philadelphus x virginalis* 'Dwarf Snowflake'), 109

moles, 140

Monarda didyma (bee balm), 48, *132*

Monotropa uniflora (ghost plants, Indian pipe), 137

Montauk daisy (Nippon daisy) (*Nipponanthemum nipponicum*), 22, 50, 56

mop cypress (*Chamaecyparis pisifera spp.* 'Gold Thread' 'Gold Mop'), 110

mophead hydrangea (*Hydrangea macrophylla*), 84, *90*

and climate change, 26, 28, *28*

flower colors, *86*, 87

'Glowing Embers', *84*

'Nikko Blue', *92*, 114

'Penny Mac', *84*

planting, 87–88

popularity of, 1, 83

problems with, 89–91

pruning for, 91–93, *92*

remontant varieties, 89

shade and sun for, 86, 91

and temperatures, 88–89

watering for, 85, 90

morning glory (*Ipomoea spp.*), 37

blue (*Ipomoea indica*), 39

cardinal climber (*Ipomoea sloteri*), 39

moss, *25*, 127–28

mothballs, as animal repellant, 143

mowing, 125

mugo pine (*Pinus mugo*), 111

mugwort (*Artemisia vulgaris*), 157

mulching, 8

for fruit, 67

and insects, 154

for perennials, 49–50, 53

purposes of, 10, *11*

and soil types, 7, 8

for trees, 118

for vegetables, 68, 69, 71, 75

and watering, 24

for weeds, *16*, 157

mullein (*Verbascum chaixii*), 52

mum, 22, 149

Korean (*Dendranthema spp.* 'Sheffield Pink' 'Cambodian Queen' 'Autumn Moon'), 56

Muscari armeniacum (grape hyacinth), 53

mushrooms, *25*, 137

Myrica pensylvanica (bayberry), 7, 111

Mytoi Gardens, 167

nasturtium (*Tropaeolum majus*), 35, 146

native species

groundcovers, 63

ornamental grasses, 57, 59, 60

and sandy soils, 7

trees, 118

and wildlife, 145, *156*

neem, 149, 152

nematodes, 127, 150, 152

Nepeta faassenii 'Walker's Low' (cat mint), *32*, 50, 56

New Guinea impatiens (*Impatiens hawkeri* 'Sun-Patiens'), *34*, 37, *41*, 134

Nicotiana mutabilis (flowering tobacco), 38

Nicotiana sylvestris (flowering tobacco), 38

ninebark (*Physocarpus opulifolius spp.* 'Diablo' 'Centerglow'), *106*, 109, 114, 135, *161*

Nipponanthemum nipponicum (Nippon daisy) (Montauk daisy), 22, 50, 56

Nippon daisy (Montauk daisy) (*Nipponanthemum nipponicum*), 22, 50, 56

nitrogen, 7, 36, 122, 159

Norway spruce, dwarf (*Picea abies* 'Pumila'), 110

nut sedge, 126

oak, 118

red (*Quercus rubra*), 120

white (*Quercus alba*), 120

and wildlife, 145

oakleaf hydrangea (*Hydrangea quercifolia*), 84, 97

flower colors, 87

'Pee Wee', 99

'Ruby Slippers', 99

'Snow Queen', 99

watering, 85

ocean effects, 20–22, 72, 111

Ocimum basilicum (basil), 46, 133, *133*

Ocimum sp. hybrid 'Amazel' (Italian basil), *45*, 134

Olethreutes ferriferana (hydrangea leaftier), *94*, 96–97

onion (*Allium cepa*), 73

oregano (*Origanum sp.*), 45, 149

organic amendments, 10, 71

Origanum sp. (oregano), 45, 149

ornamental grasses, 57–61

Osteospermum sp. (daisybush), 40

Oxalis triangularis (purple oxali), 38

Oxydendrum arboreum (sourwood), 120

pachysandra (Japanese spurge) (*Pachysandra*

Acknowledgments

YOU ARE READING THIS BOOK because so many people have provided me with information and encouragement in the years I've been gardening on the Cape. From all the generous fellow gardeners to area plant experts, I've been fortunate to benefit from their knowledge and support. The Cape and Islands are filled with lovely gardens and I am privileged that so many have welcomed me to their landscapes and agreed to have photos of their gardens included here.

Of equal importance have been the gardeners and home landscapers that ask me questions; whether they've called GardenLine on WXTK, spoken to me at Hyannis Country Garden, or had me consult on their property, these folks have helped me to understand what *they* need to know. Those conversations have led to some of the material for this book.

The crew at David R. Godine, Publisher has my sincere appreciation as well: Sue Berger Ramin and David Godine for being willing to so quickly say "yes" when I proposed this book; Sara Eisenman for the lovely design; Ally Findley for her careful editing; and Kim Courchesne and Michael Babcock for their sales and production expertise respectively. The Red Sox aren't the only ones with a winning Boston lineup this year, and I'm grateful to have Team Godine in my corner.

Finally, a shout out to GardenComm, Garden Communicators International. This organization has been an important network for me as a garden writer and speaker; I've been blessed to be a member of a group that is dedicated to cultivating each other and horticulture in general. They are truly growing greater good.

COLOPHON

Designed by John Bell of London, *Bell* was the contemporary of and influenced by the French designs Didot and Fournier, as well as the neoclassical typeface, Baskerville. The matrixes for Bell were cut in London in 1788 by Richard Austin. In 1864, Henry Oscar Houghton brought Bell to Boston, where it became quite popular with Bruce Rogers of the Riverside Press, but under the new name Brimmer. Stanley Morison added Bell to the Monotype Corporation Library in 1931. To quote Robert Bringhurst: "The serif's are very sharp, but the overall spirit is nevertheless closer to brick than to granite, evoking Lincoln's Inn more than St Paul's, and Harvard Yard more than Pennsylvania Avenue. Bell numerals are three-quarter height, neither hanging nor fully ranging."

This book was designed and typeset by Sara Eisenman